OVERWORKED AND UNDERPAID

THE LIFE OF AN ELECTION OFFICIAL

E. Randall Wertz

ISBN 978-1-64300-800-4 (Paperback)
ISBN 978-1-64300-801-1 (Digital)

Covenant Books, Inc.
11661 Hwy 707
Murrells Inlet, SC 29576
www.covenantbooks.com

Without a doubt there is only one person
this book can be dedicated to:

Mercedes "Marcy" Leon Wertz, my beautiful,
intelligent, loving, and caring wife!
As they say on many Valentine's Day items,
"I wish my wife could see herself
through my eyes because then she could
see how much she means to me."
Marcy means everything to me. She is the greatest
wife in the world and my best friend.
There is no one else I would rather spend my time with.
Thank you, Marcy! I love you!

"This is so sad that they have to drag Juanita's name through the mud when she has passed on and can't defend herself. If those writing these stories only knew half of what we as registrars have to do and are responsible for then they might see it differently. It is a daily struggle but we just keep pushing through . . . that's just what we do . . . what other choice do we have? I thank the good Lord every day for my friends and coworkers . . . the other 132 registrars." Ms. Tiney Thompson Rose, General Registrar in Alleghany County, said this on Facebook when the Voter Registrars Association of Virginia President, Walt Latham, said, "I am really getting tired of hearing or reading the former Fredericksburg registrar being described as a rogue registrar."

I recently retired from the election business and thought I would write something to enlighten the news media and other individuals who are so anxious to complain and condemn us when something goes wrong in an election. There are sections of this book that will probably cause you to yawn because they cover what we do. These duties are extensive and detailed. So please bear with me, and I think you might enjoy some of the stories my colleagues and I have to share. Politics is a difficult business today because the country is definitely split in half, and no matter what we did we were sure to make someone unhappy. Buckle your seat belt, it is going to be a bumpy ride. Hopefully, when I finish, you will have a new appreciation for these hardworking and underpaid professionals.

Let me begin by providing some background on how I got into this business. I graduated from the "true university of Virginia—Virginia Tech," with a BA degree in History. Immediately after graduation I moved to the City of Danville, Virginia where I taught and coached in the public school system. I thoroughly enjoyed the teaching and coaching, but I did not enjoy the salary I was being paid. My starting ten-month salary was $7,200. After three years, my salary increased to $8,500 and that included my coaching supplement. So, I started looking into changing careers and was fortunate enough to have an administrator in a small hospital in Southwest Virginia offer me the hospital's first Personnel Director's job. Therefore, as a result, I spent most of my career providing human resource services in industry and healthcare. As the Director of Human Resources in many of these facilities, I was also given responsibility for marketing, public relations, public facilities management, and information technology. All these experiences prepared me for the challenge of working in the elections community.

While working for Hampshire Designers, Inc., a knitting manufacturer in Virginia, I learned of an opening in Montgomery County, where Virginia Tech, my alma mater, is located. The County Administrator, Ms. Betty S. Thomas, was looking for someone with human resources experience for their Deputy Assistant County Administrator position. This position would also be responsible for the human services, parks and recreation departments, as well as rural additions (roads). I jumped at the chance to get back near Virginia Tech and to support the Hokies. While in this position I became familiar with all aspects of Montgomery County government and with the road experience, I got to know the four distinct districts that make up this growing community: Blacksburg, Christiansburg, Riner, Shawsville and Elliston. I thoroughly enjoyed this position, but there was a change in county administrators and the new one had a totally different vision. As a result, I left to take another Human Resources Director position with a diabetic supply company in Roanoke, Virginia.

A few years later, the General Registrar for Montgomery County decided to retire, and the Electoral Board advertised for her position. I wanted to return to county government, so I applied. The Electoral Board is structured to have the governor's party as the majority party on the board. At that time Virginia had a democratic governor and, as a result, there were two democrats on the three-member board.

The Electoral Board showed how smart they were by selecting me for the position.

I became the General Registrar for Montgomery County on April 1, 2004. Yes, I started on April Fools' Day. This should have prepared me for what was to come. Even though I had an idea of what was really in store for me, I was not prepared for the magnitude of and dramatic changes in elections that was ahead. I hope this journey, and the experiences of my colleagues and I, will make it very clear that we do work more than a couple of days a year and are unappreciated for what we do.

CHAPTER ONE

Montgomery County's Voter Registration Office

The Commonwealth of Virginia has a unique structure for its election officials. The electoral board and general registrar are specifically mentioned in Virginia's Constitution. The founders knew the importance of these positions and wanted to make sure they did what was best for the citizens and they protected each person's vote. How did they do this? Here's how:

The Electoral Board is made up of three members. They represent the two political parties with the highest votes in our general elections. Naturally this is generally the Democratic and Republican parties. In my time as general registrar, we never had a third party get enough votes to change this makeup.

The board members serve three-year terms that are staggered. When one term ends the party chair will send three names to the circuit court judges for consideration. The first name on the list is considered by the judges as the party's selection. In my time as general registrar, the judges always went with the first name on the list. Now this can change when the governor's party changes. Let's say a Republican governor is chosen. When the next Democratic board member's term ends, he or she will be replaced by a Republican.

As mentioned earlier, when I was first selected for this position, there was a Democratic governor. As a result, two members of the electoral board were Democrats and one Republican. This makeup changed back and forth over the years. Their duties are specifically listed in Section 24.2, Article 3 of the Code of Virginia. One of these responsibilities is to hire and perform an annual performance review of the general registrar. The other responsibilities revolve around simply making elections fair and voter friendly. They work with the director of elections/general registrar to make sure the policies and procedures are clearly outlined and the staff and officers of election, who run the elections, know them and carry them out.

The office staff included a deputy assistant registrar, and two assistant registrars. So, we had a total of four (4) full-time equivalents (FTEs) serving a population of almost 100,000. One of the unique components of Montgomery County is that it also has one of the largest universities within its boundaries—Virginia Tech. This created 25 to 50 percent more work for us than in Roanoke County with a similar population. Therefore, we had a lot of work created by the students including registrations, transfers in and out, name changes, address changes, etc. Even though I was a graduate of this fine university, I joked with other registrars from the region and tried to get someone to take Virginia Tech, but no one wanted them. They knew the magnitude of work it created for us. I also oversaw the creation of two polling places on Tech's campus. I will provide more information on this matter when I start getting into the issues I experienced over the years.

Officers of election are another group I need to mention. They conduct the elections on Election Day. The number of officers of election fluctuated over the years. We normally had between 185 and 225 volunteers. And I do mean volunteers because what we paid them was nothing for the work they had to perform. When I retired, we were paying the officers of election $125 for Election Day and $25 for the training sessions they had to sit through before each election. The chief officers, who run the polling place, received $150, $25 for training and mileage for coming to my office to get their election materials the day before the election and returning them the day after the election. On Election Day they must be at the polling place by 5:00 a.m. at the latest and will work after the polls close at 7:00 p.m. until the machines are secured, paperwork completed, and results called into my office. In other words, they had to stay until 9:00 to 10:00 p.m. That's a long day for this small payment. These individuals are truly patriotic, community-minded saints. They deserve recognition and much, much more compensation for their contributions.

This is the makeup of the Elections Department. There are a small number of people who protect democracy in Montgomery County. This is just one of 133 other counties and cities across our great Commonwealth of Virginia. Each one is different because of the number of registered voters, but they must all do the same work by following the Code of Virginia and the rules and regulations established by the Virginia Department of Elections.

The part-time and full-time members of my staff were: Glenna Mitchell, Freda Alderman, Amber Yopp, Gary Talkington, Connie Viar and Charles "Zeke" Bleakley. Glenna and Freda are the longest tenured in the office. Freda retired after the 2011 General Election with over twenty-five years of service. Without her knowledge and guidance, I would have had a very difficult first year because I had town elections and a presidential election in that year; I owe her a lot and we are still close friends.

Glenna Mitchell was in the office when I became the general registrar. She was considered a loner. She chose to keep her personal life to herself and was not what you would call outgoing. As with Freda, she had a ton of historical knowledge that was very beneficial. She and Freda, however, would have arguments all the time because of their opposite personalities. Glenna would not take much time off and was very possessive regarding her job duties. She was not comfortable taking on additional duties. I had to be very careful in what assignments I gave out due to these limitations. Glenna is still working in the office and will probably be there until she passes away.

Freda Alderman was the perfect employee. She was dedicated, knew every aspect of her job, kept learning as much as she could about the Code of Virginia, was level headed, and very loyal. She was also a great sounding board. Everyone in the other regional offices and at State Board loved her because of how she interacted with them. Freda was the employee you wished you could clone. When she retired, a huge hole was left in the office because I lost her historical knowledge and her daily encouragement. As I said earlier, I would have had a much more difficult time adjusting to my responsibilities without her assistance. She and her husband, Sammy, were two good Christians and helped keep me on the right path with their sage advice.

At the time I came aboard, there was a young lady working as an assistant registrar. Her name was Amber Yopp. Amber was in her early twenties and was married to a young minister at one of the local churches. Her family was in Roanoke, and she wanted to move closer to them. She and her husband moved to Roanoke within a few months and she went to work for the Roanoke City Library.

Gary Talkington was a dedicated employee. I first met Gary when he walked into my office while attending Radford University and asked to be an intern. Not many college students want to intern in our office because we have a finite number of staff and there isn't much money in our field. It was also unique because Gary was an older student. He was a year older than me. Gary and I spoke for quite a while that day, and I decided to give him a try. At that time, I did not have an open position because County Administration had frozen my second assistant registrar position due to the county's financial situation. So, an intern position was the only option. Thankfully, it worked out for both of us. When he started, I gave him the Code of Virginia and the General Registrar and Electoral Board Handbook to read and absorb. Gary did very well on this and had several good questions on why certain laws and procedures were in place. Because of his computer knowledge I had him help me with the electronic pollbooks and voting machines. I certainly needed his assistance because I had to deal with them myself while also preparing for an election. This responsibility was taking its toll on me physically, so I was very happy to have this help. We worked very well together as a team and accomplished quite a bit including training of our officers of elections on the new machines. Finally, after a lot of complaining on my part, County Administration allowed me to hire a part-time assistant registrar. I immediately moved Gary into this position. Eventually, I was permitted to increase it to a full-time position. When this happened, I was able to turn over the electronic pollbooks and voting machines to Gary and I could concentrate on preparing for the elections. Unfortunately, Gary started experiencing some health issues and eventually retired per his physician's recommendation. He got involved with the Blacksburg Rotary Club and the Montgomery County Republican Party, but his health kept deteriorating and he eventually passed away in 2017. To the very end he was a good friend and very loyal.

When Gary retired, I advertised his position and hired Charles "Zeke" Bleakley to replace him. Zeke came to us from the Post Office. Prior to this position, he was in the navy. While in the navy he worked on the electronic equipment on ships. Therefore, his move into a position dealing with electronic pollbooks and voting machines was logical. Zeke also worked well with our officers of election. Some liked him so much that they wrote glowing statements about him on our training evaluation forms. Zeke's one drawback was his quick response that "everything is under control." I kept warning him that he needed to check and double-check things because in our line of work, if something can go wrong it will. I am sure this will sink in eventually. Hopefully before he makes a major mistake.

When Zeke came aboard, I trained him the same way as Gary, and he adjusted well. I also asked him to come up with a better way to provide information to our chief officers during Election Day. He used a notebook and an accordion file to do so and he did a great job. The chief officers were very appreciative of this effort.

The last person I need to mention is Ms. Connie Viar. Just before Freda Alderman retired, I advertised her position and interviewed several qualified applicants. I chose Ms. Viar because she had been the clerk of the Juvenile and Domestic Relations Court in Montgomery County. In this position she knew how to read and interpret the Code of Virginia and had supervised other staff members. She missed her first day of work due to illness and it just happened to be Election Day. So, she missed her first election. I had hoped she would get to sit back and watch what went on, so she would get an overall view of how an election is run. She came in on the day after the election and got to see what we do after the election. It wasn't as good as seeing the full election, but it had to do. I told Connie that I thought she, once she gets the training and experience, would be a natural fit in my position. I did what I could to expose her to all aspects of the office and my position. When I announced I was planning to retire, the electoral board asked me to stay on through the 2016 Presidential Election. I said I would and scheduled to retire on March 1, 2017. After the presidential election, the electoral board advertised for my position and interviewed several applicants. I wrote a letter to the electoral board on Ms. Viar's behalf, recommending her for the position.

I would be remiss if I didn't mention a very special person who worked for us on a temporary basis—Gloria Craighead. She came to work for us before the 2016 Presidential Election. It was hard finding someone that really wanted to work through Bright Services. They sent us several other people, but these temps couldn't concentrate on the jobs we had for them and, in some cases, didn't show up as scheduled. They sent us Gloria. From the first day, her personality was infectious. She would do any job, including voter registration form filing, and she did it without any complaining and wanted to learn as much as possible about everything in the office to help us. She was perfect for what we needed. Unfortunately, we were not as fortunate with the others sent to us. As Gloria became more familiar with our duties, she answered the phones, covered the front counter, and entered data into the database system (VERIS). She learned quickly and provided great support while she was with us. Gloria's greatest trait was her ability to deal with the public. Gloria could change the customer's attitude by showing them that she really did want to help them. As you will see later, at times the public is not very friendly when they come to our office. Some were really hostile, and Gloria could melt that hostility within a few minutes by being empathetic and using her southern country charm.

If I weren't going to retire, I would have done everything I could to keep her with us. Since I was leaving at the end of February 2017, I left that decision to my successor, Connie Viar, my Deputy Assistant Registrar. Once I went with Connie to the HR Director to start the process I stepped back and let her control the hiring process.

Connie chose not to interview Gloria. Obviously, I don't know how the employee she chose has worked out, but I feel she missed an opportunity to keep a person who worked well with everyone, knew the office, and could hit the ground running instead of having to train a new employee. In my opinion it was an opportunity missed.

I was very blessed to have such a diverse group of staff members. Even though we had totally different personalities, skills, and abilities, when elections took place we worked well as a team and were able to get a lot accomplished.

CHAPTER TWO

Duties and Powers of the General Registrar/Director of Elections.

Now let's determine what a director of elections/general registrar does. To get this, we must go to the Code of Virginia, Section 24.2-114. Please do not fall asleep on me as you read this, but it is necessary:

"§ 24.2-114. Duties and powers of the General Registrar.

In addition to the other duties required by this title, the general registrar, and the assistant registrars acting under his supervision, shall:

1. Maintain the office of the general registrar and establish and maintain additional public places for voter registration in accordance with the provisions of § 24.2-412.
2. Participate in programs to educate the general public concerning registration and encourage registration by the general public. No registrar shall actively solicit, in a selective manner, any application for registration or for a ballot or offer anything of value for any such application.
3. Perform his duties within the county or city he was appointed to serve, except that a registrar may (i) go into a county or city in the Commonwealth contiguous to his county or city to register voters of his county or city when

conducting registration jointly with the registrar of the contiguous county or city or (ii) notwithstanding any other provision of law, participate in multijurisdictional staffing for voter registration offices, approved by the State Board, that are located at facilities of the Department of Motor Vehicles.

4. Provide the appropriate forms for applications to register and to obtain the information necessary to complete the applications pursuant to the provisions of the Constitution of Virginia and general law.

5. Indicate on the registration records for each accepted mail voter registration application form returned by mail pursuant to Article 3.1 (§ 24.2-416.1 et seq.) of Chapter 4 that the registrant has registered by mail. The general registrar shall fulfill this duty in accordance with the instructions of the State Board so that those persons who registered by mail are identified on the registration records, lists of registered voters furnished pursuant to § 24.2-405, lists of persons who voted furnished pursuant to § 24.2-406, and pollbooks used for the conduct of elections.

6. Accept a registration application or request for transfer or change of address submitted by or for a resident of any other county or city in the Commonwealth. Registrars shall process registration applications and requests for transfer or change of address from residents of other counties and cities in accordance with written instructions from the State Board and shall forward the completed application or request to the registrar of the applicant's residence. Notwithstanding the provisions of § 24.2-416, the registrar of the applicant's residence shall recognize as timely any application or request for transfer or change of address submitted to any person authorized to receive voter registration applications pursuant to Chapter 4 (§ 24.2-400 et seq.), prior to or on the final day of registration. The registrar of the applicant's residence shall determine the qualification of the applicant, including whether the appli-

cant has ever been convicted of a felony, and if so, under what circumstances the applicant's right to vote has been restored, and promptly notify the applicant at the address shown on the application or request of the acceptance or denial of his registration or transfer. However, notification shall not be required when the registrar does not have an address for the applicant.

7. Preserve order at and in the vicinity of the place of registration. For this purpose, the registrar shall be vested with the powers of a conservator of the peace while engaged in the duties imposed by law. He may exclude from the place of registration persons whose presence disturbs the registration process. He may appoint special officers, not exceeding three in number, for a place of registration and may summon persons in the vicinity to assist whenever, in his judgment, it is necessary to preserve order. The general registrar and any assistant registrar shall be authorized to administer oaths for purposes of this title.

8. Maintain the official registration records for his county or city in the system approved by, and in accordance with the instructions of, the State Board; preserve the written applications of all persons who are registered; and preserve for a period of four years the written applications of all persons who are denied registration or whose registration is cancelled.

9. If a person is denied registration, promptly notify such person in writing of the denial and the reason for denial in accordance with § 24.2-422.

10. Verify the accuracy of the pollbooks provided for each election by the State Board, make the pollbooks available to the precincts, and according to the instructions of the State Board provide a copy of the data from the pollbooks to the State Board after each election for voting credit purposes.

11. Retain the pollbooks in his principal office for two years from the date of the election.

12. Maintain accurate and current registration records and comply with the requirements of this title for the transfer, inactivation, and cancellation of voter registrations.
13. Whenever election districts, precincts, or polling places are altered, provide for entry into the voter registration system of the proper district and precinct designations for each registered voter whose districts or precinct have changed and notify each affected voter of changes affecting his districts or polling place by mail.
14. Whenever any part of his county or city becomes part of another jurisdiction by annexation, mergers, or other means, transfer to the appropriate general registrar the registration records of the affected registered voters. The general registrar for their new county or city shall notify them by mail of the transfer and their new election districts and polling places.
15. When he registers any person who was previously registered in another state, notify the appropriate authority in that state of the person's registration in Virginia by providing electronically, through the Department of Elections, the information contained in that person's registration application.
16. Whenever any person is believed to be registered or voting in more than one state or territory of the United States at the same time, inquire about, or provide information from the voter's registration and voting records to any appropriate voter registration or other authority of another state or territory who inquires about, that person's registration and voting history.
17. At the request of the county or city chairman of any political party nominating a candidate for the General Assembly, constitutional office, or local office by a method other than a primary, review any petition required by the party in its nomination process to determine whether those signing the petition are registered voters with active status.

18. Carry out such other duties as prescribed by the electoral board in his capacity as the director of elections for the locality in which he serves.

19. Attend an annual training program provided by the State Board. A general registrar may designate one member of his staff to attend such training program if he is unable to attend because of a personal or family emergency.

Code 1950, §§ 24-59, 24-60, 24-60.1, 24-71 through 24-73, 24-90, 24-93, 24-94, 24-101, 24-111, 24-115, 24-118; 1950, p. 381; 1958, c. 576; 1962, cc. 422, 536; 1968, c. 143; 1970, c. 462, §§ 24.1-46, 24.1-54, 24.1-68; 1972, c. 620; 1973, c. 30; 1974, c. 428; 1976, c. 616; 1979, c. 329; 1980, c. 639; 1982, c. 650; 1983, c. 398; 1984, c. 480; 1986, c. 558; 1990, c. 193; 1993, c. 641; 1996, cc. 72, 73; 1998, c. 354; 2000, cc. 512, 556, 857; 2003, c. 1015; 2005, c. 380; 2010, c. 812; 2013, c. 491; 2015, cc. 644, 645; 2016, cc. 13, 633.

The chapters of the acts of assembly referenced in the historical citation at the end of this section may not constitute a comprehensive list of such chapters and may exclude chapters whose provisions have expired."

Number 18 is the key paragraph, and this varies over the entire Commonwealth of Virginia: "18. Carry out such other duties as prescribed by the electoral board in his capacity as the director of elections for the locality in which he serves." The Commonwealth has 133 cities and counties. They obviously range in size, and so the responsibilities of the director of elections/general registrar vary in each one. The responsibilities are also determined by the activity or inactivity of the electoral board. My board was very active and wanted to be involved in everything, so my responsibilities included keeping them apprised of everything that occurred and any communications from the Department of Elections. Plus, it was imperative that I keep them informed of each step of a process. In some localities

the electoral boards did not want to be involved and let the director of elections/general registrar do everything. I was envious of these GRs. Obviously both options have their positives and negatives.
When we were working together my board and I were very successful and accomplished a lot for the citizens of Montgomery County. But when we didn't, things "went to hell in a handbasket." The first couple of boards I had were less active and, as a result, we had one focus. When my boards started to become more and more active, and wanted to promote their own agendas, it became harder and harder for me to keep us focused. I will mention some specific incidents a little later in the book.

The Local Electoral Board

The local electoral board is made up of three members. In Virginia two of the members are from the governor's party and the third member from the opposing party. When I retired, Virginia had a Democrat Governor so two members were Democrat and the third member was Republican. Normally, one of the majority party members is the board's secretary and the single party member becomes the chairman. The second majority party member becomes the vice chairman. However, this can change if no one from the majority party wants the extra responsibilities. The extra duties include taking and printing the minutes of the meetings and performing any additional clerical duties required. The board votes on this every March.

During the majority of my tenure, I had good boards who cared about the voters and did not let party affiliation affect their decisions on the board. However, I also had some boards who could not refrain from bringing party politics into our meetings and their directions to me. Obviously, this created animosity and distrust between everyone, but it is the nature of politics.

My first board was made up of the following members: Brenda Eanes (D), Dean Dowdy (R), and Rosalie Paige (D). This board was a great board. Not only did they show their intelligence by hiring me, but we had to deal with a myriad of issues and the requirement of our voting machines. These outstanding individuals worked tirelessly on behalf of the citizens of Montgomery County. They also had to provide encouragement to a new GR while facing two town elections within a month of my appointment and an impending presidential election in November. This board took a lot of abuse for doing the right thing and deserve a lot more recognition than they have received. The first abuse came from my Democratic Party members' party chair. He was upset because he had specifically told them who to hire for my position. He wanted a Democrat in the position, so they could control the elections. His demand shows how much he knew about our jobs and the first requirement that we must be non-partisan in our action. But they still took the abuse and stood by their action.

Their next hard decision was what to do about our aging voting equipment. The Help America Vote Act passed by Congress in 2002 told us that we had to eliminate our lever machines ASAP and get new machines. The Virginia State Board of Elections started working on this and provided six machines for us to pick from. The board and I started to work on this and developed a review committee that included the department staff and an additional member Randall Gwinn, a member of the IT Department. We eliminated two of the machines immediately because one had received very bad press and had been bashed by Black Box Voting for its failures. The other machine was extremely old technology and used dummy terminals for people to vote on. We received presentations from the other four vendors: Advanced Voting Solutions (AVS), Election Systems and Software (ES&S), Hart Voting Solutions, and Sequoia Voting Solutions. After all of the interviews, I provided each member of the committee with an evaluation sheet for each machine and asked them to rank them. We also included customer service as one of the evaluation measures. It was very clear by reviewing the evaluation that Advanced Voting Solutions WINvote machine was the best. So, when the electoral board decided to make a decision and place their choice in the minutes of their meeting, we notified the public and we had a large turnout for the meeting. It was heavily attended by those who were against any touchscreen machines and against changing from the lever machines. They were very vocal in their opposition and included members of the League of Women Voters and the Democratic Party Chair. But they failed to recognize our dilemma that we had to move quickly or we would lose the $225,000 we would get from the Help America Vote Act. The citizens of Montgomery County would have been stuck with the bill for new machines. Our lever machines were being held together by rubber bands and chewing gum at this point and we had to move forward. So, the Board voted to go with the WINvote machines and present this to the board of supervisors.

Over the years as governors changed and members decided to retire or were asked to leave by their parties, I had new boards to deal with. Some worked well together, some didn't. There was one situation when they failed to check with me prior to making a decision during an election and this created a major problem for voting and for all of us. This happened in the November 2010 General Election. We were rolling out new electronic pollbooks and six of our twenty-two precincts failed to open them properly. So, I was on the phone helping them get started, when Precinct E-1 called in just before the polls were to open and asked what to do. One of the board members, Cynthia Chappelka (D), spoke with Helen Young

(R) and they told the chief officer to use a note pad and take down the names of people voting. This was not the correct procedure. We were supposed to provide the voters with provisional ballots to be placed in envelopes. Then once the election was over they would be counted once they could be verified as eligible voters. This failure to follow procedures got the board and I investigated by the Attorney General's Office and after their recommendation, censured by the State Board of Elections. All of this could have been prevented if the board members had simply walked into my office and asked what to do. The *Roanoke Times* took great pleasure in this censure and wrote a large article criticizing me. This is a prime example of even though we are not responsible, general registrars/directors of elections are always blamed. And we cannot fight back because they have unlimited amounts of ink and we cannot win.

I do need to mention at this time that the members of the Voter Registrars Association of Virginia are a great group of professionals. They came out in great numbers to support me at the State Board of Elections meeting. They understood my situation and that they could be in it too. My dear friends Barbara Gunter (Bedford County), Dana Oliver (Salem City), Kay Chitwood (Franklin County), and Frances Ragland (Goochland County) were very supportive, as were many more. This was a very difficult time for me and they were there for me. I can't thank them enough.

I also need to recognize another board member who represented the best in what they should be—John Nowlin. John was a gentleman and studied the Code and the GR/EB Handbook. He totally worked on behalf of the voters and would do anything to do what is best. He was also a stabilizing/calming force on the board. When the board meeting got heated, he could always be counted on to calm things down. He always voted by using that great commodity—common sense. I am indebted to him for making very tense situations bearable. Even after leaving the board, he has remained a friend.

Although I had boards that never got along, I have never had to deal with one that was totally against me. However, several GRs have had to deal with this. I can only imagine how difficult it would be to get your job done during this situation. Some of these disagreements have been political and others have been personal. The political ones have generally been settled in court and generally in favor of the GR. The personal ones have generally been over power struggles and in these situations the board wins.

The bottom line is that electoral boards can be good and bad for GRs. If they are all on the same page and they let the GR do his/her job, then everything is great, and you get a lot accomplished. When the board wants to control everything and stands over the GR, nothing but bad things can happen. The GR must have freedom to run the office and voter registration, manage the staff, deal with the public, and prepare for elections without interference. Unfortunately, some boards can't help themselves and want to hang around the office and get the staff to do special projects for them. I have had them, and they are toxic.

Here is a list of my electoral board members from my twelve plus years of service and their party affiliations: Dean Dowdy (R), Brenda Eanes (D), Rosalie Paige (D), Cynthia Chappelka (D), John Nowlin (D), Helen Young (R), Richard Langford (R), Carroll Williams (D), Freddie McKenzie, and John Sills (D). Mr. Sills came in just before I left and replaced Mr. McKenzie who resigned. As you can see there have been more Democrats than Republicans. This occurred because there were more Democratic governors; the Democratic Party chair wanted to remove some members because they did not follow his orders, and some had had enough. Being an electoral board member is not as easy as many have been told—especially in a county as divided as Montgomery County. Many of my board members were told they would just have to meet a couple of times a year but because of the constant changes in election laws, the proactive public in Montgomery County, and contentious elections this is not possible. Some get worn out while others turn this into their work and they show up almost every day. My position is that those who show up almost every day tend to get too involved in the daily operation and create problems for the GR. My personal experiences back this up. You can tell working with the electoral board is like walking a tightrope. You must be very careful, keep your balance, and concentrate on not falling off.

In order to counter Secretary of the State Board Nancy Rodrigues's grab for power, the Voter Registrars Association of Virginia (VRAV) recommended the use of an annual review by the local electoral board. My board had been doing this before this directive for the Montgomery County Human Resources Department. They now had two evaluations to do. Dean Dowdy went to the HR Director and asked if they could just do one for both and she agreed. The one for the SBE was due July 1 and the one for the County was due in April. They agreed on the July date. The performance evaluations were graded on a scale of 1 (Not Meeting Expectations) to 5 (Exceeding Expectations). Until Carroll Williams came on the board I always received all 5s. But even with her negative comments, the lowest score I received was 4.5. I am proud of the work I did, and my boards recognized that I went beyond the call of duty. I guess I was a pretty good tightrope walker.

Voting Machines and Electronic Pollbooks

When I took over as general registrar in 2004, Montgomery County was using a lever machine made by the Shoup Voting Machine Corporation. A picture of this machine is shown below. It was a monster of a machine. Our Buildings and Grounds staff was exhausted at the end of the day after delivering them to our polling places.

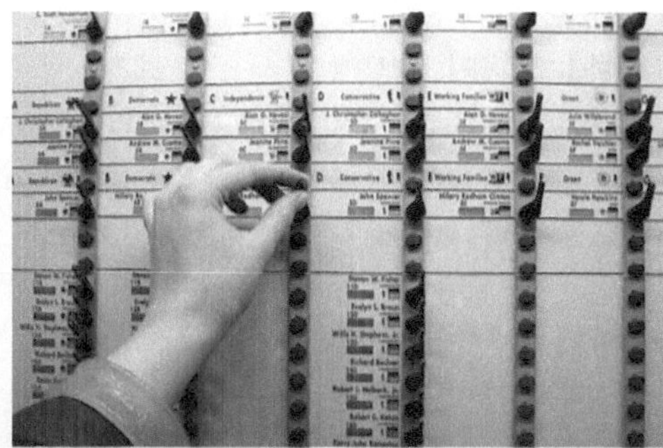

"Safemaker Jacob H. Meyers created the Automatic Voting Machine in 1888 and established the Automatic Voting Machine Corporation (AVM) in 1898. Samuel R. Shoup followed his example, built his own lever voting machine and founded the Shoup Voting Machine Corporation in 1905. It 'operated on a limited scale,' until 'the development and sale of the model 2.5 in the mid-1930s turned the corporation into a successful and profitable operation.' The two rivals grew to dominate the American market. By 1928, one of six citizens registered their votes on an AVM or Shoup machine. In all, Shoup sold 100,000 lever-operated voting machines, half of which were still working and in use for the 2000 presidential election."

This machine was mechanical and very easy to operate by the voter. As we discovered when we finally had to go to touch screen machines, the voter really missed the "ding" the machine made when the voters recorded their votes and opened the curtain on the machine. This sound was reassuring to the voter. Our voters loved this machine and frankly would have been happy to continue with them except we had the "hanging chads" in Florida during the 2000 Presidential Election.

After the 2000 Presidential Election, the psyche of the public changed nationwide, and a good portion of voters started to distrust the election community. They started calling for changes within elections and the politicians in Congress were more than happy to ride in on the white horse and save the day! As a result, Congress passed the Help America Vote Act (HAVA) in 2002. This law provided new regulations to help voters feel more comfortable with how elections were run by mandating that all in-person voting would have to be done electronically to avoid the chaos of hanging chads and butterfly ballots. HAVA requires states to use funding to replace punched card voting systems or lever voting systems with new systems in accordance with HAVA's voting system standards.

"HAVA set forth requirements for all voting systems, including that they:

- permit the voter to verify (in a private and independent manner) the votes selected by the voter on the ballot before the ballot is cast and counted;
- provide the voter with the opportunity (in a private and independent manner) to change the ballot or correct any error before the ballot is cast and counted (including the opportunity to correct the error through the issuance of a replacement ballot if the voter was otherwise unable to change the ballot or correct any error); and
- Notify the voter of overvotes (votes for more than the maximum number of selections allowed in a contest) and provide the voter a chance to correct these errors.
- States that do not use electronic equipment to assist voters with detecting errors must:
- establish a voter education program, specific to that voting system, that notifies each voter of the effect of casting multiple votes for an office; and
- Provide the voter with instructions on how to correct the ballot before it is cast and counted.

HAVA further requires that any required notification preserve the privacy of the voter and the secrecy of the ballot; and that alternative-language accessibility be available pursuant to the requirements of section 203 of the Voting Rights Act."

For election officials, a key component of the legislation was the $3.9 billion set aside for states to purchase new voting machines. In Virginia, the Department of Elections—known as the State Board of Elections at that time (SBE), decided to distribute the money to the various localities based on the number of registered voters. We were a medium-sized locality and received approximately $212,000 from SBE. This allowed us to purchase the new voting machines and some of the supplies we needed to run them.

At that time the State Board of Elections approved six different touch screen machines for us to select from. They were all about the same cost and it was left up to the locality to choose the machine best for them. I set up a committee to review demonstrations from the vendors we were interested in interviewing. I made sure that we had a representative from the IT Department (Randal Gwinn) because of the technology we were reviewing. He was an outstanding addition to the committee and provided valuable insight to the other members. He told us whether the technology was old or new. He also guided us on the makeup of the machine and if it would provide us many years of service. Randal was and is a strong supporter of our department.

We automatically deleted one of the machines, Diebold, because of the history of errors and bad programming. There was also a very vocal group of people from Blacksburg totally against touch screen electronic equipment because they were listening to Black Box Voting and Verified Voting who were strongly against the Diebold machine. I did not want to fight this group and ended up interviewing the following vendors: Advanced Voting Solutions (AVS), Election Services and Software (ES&S), Hart Voting, and Sequoia Voting Systems.

Each member of the committee did their own evaluation of each of the machines; it was the Advanced Voting Solutions (AVS) machine (WINvote) that came out on top. It not only had the newest technology but it was also very easy to use for voters with disabilities.

Plus, it had wireless capabilities that would make it easier to program for elections and start up and shut down by the officers of election on Election Day. The AVS salesperson (Kimberlee Shoup) was also very knowledgeable of the machine, seemed to really care about doing what was best for Montgomery County, was easy to work with, and provided extensive information on the machines for our evaluation.

Before I go any further, however, I want to recognize an individual who I consider the most knowledgeable person on Virginia elections and politics—Spooner Hull. Spooner is the owner of Atlantic Election Services (AES) and provided the service on our Shoup lever machines. I had to think long and hard about leaving AES because of Spooner's dedication to Montgomery County and knowledge of elections in general. He would do everything for the general registrars he worked for. He would assist in determining the number of ballots needed, assist in the setup of the ballot for them, and load the ballots on the machines with minimal supervision. He could be trusted on every aspect of the voting machines, the makeup of the ballot, and making sure the programming of the machines was done accurately. I hated to give this customer service up but the AVS machine was the newest technology and could be trusted for a longer service life. We had to do what was best for the voters of Montgomery County and I think we did. But I owe Spooner a lot because of his guidance and friendship during the early months of my tenure. Thanks Spooner—you are a true Southern gentleman and are the most knowledgeable man I know on Virginia elections.

I will continue on the election machine journey. The Blacksburg group against touch screen machines (DREs) continued to protest against the WINvote machines and showed up in numbers when the electoral board met to vote on which machine to purchase. The electoral board knew that if we did not move forward with the purchase of these machines that we could lose the HAVA money available to us. We also had our lever machines falling apart and would have to replace them soon. They voted unanimously to purchase the WINvote machines. Those against the touch screen machines continued to protest the purchase of these machines during the public hearing held by the board of supervisors. The board of supervisors, after much discussion, allowed us to purchase twenty-four machines to set up at a future election so that voters could become familiar with them and the board could see the voters' reaction before we bought the remaining one hundred and twenty-one machines.

We purchased the twenty-four and demonstrated the machines during the next election. The only negative comments were from the elderly who were intimidated by the technology. The younger voters and those knowledgeable with computers loved the machines because they were so easy to use. The voters with disabilities also fell in love with the machines because they could vote on the same machines as other voters. I even received an email from a disabled voter who expressed her joy at voting like everyone else. Once we bought the remaining machines and used them for an actual election, we heard only positive comments on the machines.

The opposition to these machines grew across the Commonwealth and a small group within the general assembly took up the cause to prevent their future purchase. It took several years but they finally convinced enough general assembly members to vote to keep localities from purchasing any more DREs.

A few years into this process, the Secretary of the State Board of Elections (Donald L. Palmer) saw the writing on the wall and recommended to all of us at our annual training session that we needed to start moving toward purchasing optical scan machines. He also made it clear that the general assembly would not be providing any funding like the HAVA money. It would be up to the localities to come up with the funding for the new machines. Obviously with state and local funding down and the economy not doing well, this would be a monumental task. Secretary Palmer was very wise and gave us plenty of time to get prepared before the 2016 Presidential Election.

I came up with the plan of spreading the cost over a three-year period. In doing so we could spread the total cost over this period and we could introduce them to a smaller number of precincts at one time. With twenty-four precincts, we could introduce them in eight precincts each year. This way we could also have plenty for training sessions, news releases, and news segments on how to use the ballots and the machines.

The County Administrator, Craig Meadows, saw how this could work and understood we needed to do this sooner than later.

As a result, he gave his blessing to this and included this funding in our budget requests over the next three (3) years. The board of supervisors approved this request, along with the request to get new electronic pollbooks over the same period. This way we would have all new machines and be ahead of the general assembly's schedule.

We went through the same process in selecting the new machines like we did with the WINvotes. This time I asked that a representative of the League of Women Voters be added to our decision group. I asked this because they were against the touch screen machines and if they were part of the process I hoped they would support our decision. This was a good move because it worked out as I had anticipated. Everyone agreed that we should go with the Unisyn OpenElect Voting Optical (OVO) machine. Like the WINvote machines, they were easy to operate and unlike the DREs it provided a paper trail with the paper ballot. Ms. Kimberlee Shoup-Erney, owner of Election Services Online (ESO), also provided the service contract on the machine, so we were familiar and very comfortable with her company's customer service. A picture of this machine is shown below.

The Unisyn OVO machine

In an eleven (11) year span we had three different types of voting machines—lever, touchscreen and optical scan. This was challenge enough but we had to train all our officers of election to operate each one. Just consider training 185 to 225 individuals on how to start, operate, and shut down some highly technical voting machines and to do the same with laptop computers as pollbooks. One of the factors affecting our training was that the average age of our officers of election was approximately seventy years old. Many had never used a mouse and had never worked on a laptop or desktop. The training took a lot of time and effort from me and my assistant registrar who was assigned to this duty. During this time the software for the electronic pollbooks changed many times, which required even more training. I was fortunate to have two gentlemen who were skilled in communicating with our workers. Gary Talkington and Charles "Zeke" Bleakley were assigned to work with me on this. Gary's enthusiasm and empathy for the workers helped prepare him for this. While Zeke's technical background from the navy really prepared him for this position. He was also able to communicate with the officers of election and get them to understand what was needed. His ability to bring very technical terminology down to those who have never used the machines was very beneficial. The officers loved and trusted Gary and Zeke. They were great additions to the staff for those reasons. The director of elections/general registrar must also be an educator.

I need to mention that my plan to switch to the optical scan machines when we did was also fortuitous. We received our last shipment of voting machines in July 2015. A few months after this the Virginia Department of Elections made it known to everyone that they were concerned with the WINvote machines and their wireless capability. They had a testing group look at the unit and determine if it could be hacked. They determined that it could and immediately told all WINvote users that they must find new voting machines by the general election in 2015. Many localities had not been as proactive as us and had to dole out a huge amount of money all at once. Our plan had kept us from this fate.

We were not totally out of the woods with the decertification of the WINvote machines. We had planned on using them for voters with disabilities. They were designed specifically for this and the voters with disabilities that used them loved them. We had to get the county to purchase thirty (30) Unisyn OVI machines for this purpose. If we could have kept using the WINvote machines, we would have saved $150,000.

My successor now has all of the voting machines and pollbooks she will need for a while. Unfortunately, no one knows what the future holds for elections, and optical scan machines are not perfect either. Don't be surprised if some group starts complaining about the error rate of optical scans and wants new machines. I'm just saying!

One big difference between the touch screen and the optical scan is the use, cost, and storage of the paper. With the touch screen machines the only paper used were the tapes from the machines, the statement of results (SORs) and mailed absentee ballots. The tapes were attached to the statement of results (SOR) and these results sheets (one for each precinct) and the absentee ballots could all fit into one empty paper box. Now the optical scan machines require paper ballots. The number of ballots we used went from 35,000 to 80,000 depending on the type of election. Primaries require fewer ballots because they have a much smaller turnout (2%–10%). The presidential election always brings out the most voters and, as a result, we always made sure we had one ballot for each registered voter (100%), absentee ballots (10%) and a spoilage factor of 5%.

Not only did we have a storage problem in our office, but we are required to keep the used and unused ballots for two years after each election. We resolved our storage issue by placing shelving in our conference room. The real problem is after the election the ballots must be stored in the Clerk of the Circuit Court's office. The Clerk's Office had issues with storage space until our new courthouse was built. Fortunately, the clerk thought of this in designing the new clerk's office. She planned for enough space to accommodate the new paper ballots. Now there is plenty of space to accommodate the county's growth.

Electronic Pollbooks: Back in 2004 we used simple paper poll-books. Each precinct had a simple list of its voters in alphabetical order. The officers of election manning the reception desk would simply ask the voter their full name and address and once received would search the Microsoft Excel list until they found the voter. When they were found the officer would place a number next to the voter's name. This number corresponded to their place in line. In other words, if they were the twentieth voter that day the number twenty (20) would be placed next to his or her name. The officer would mark off the corresponding number on a sheet, so we could keep up with the number of voters for that election. This number should correspond with the number of voters indicated on the voting machine.

This was a tried and true method used for decades and decades. As in everything else, we must move forward as technology advances and the number of voters increases. The State Board of Elections (SBE) decided we needed to move into electronic pollbooks. To reduce the financial impact on localities, SBE negotiated with a company to purchase used laptops and to place their pollbook software (Advocate) on it. The negotiations resulted in localities being able to purchase a used laptop and mouse, plus all of the other materials needed, e.g., router, cables, etc. for $100 per unit. We were able to go to County Administration and the board of supervisors to obtain $7,000 to purchase seventy (70) electronic pollbooks. This was an excellent approach taken by the SBE. Not only did they provide an opportunity for everyone to make the change, it also started everyone in the right direction. Now the difficult work began because my staff and I had to train our officers of election on how to use them.

This was a monumental task for us. As I mentioned, we had 185 to 225 officers to train. The average age of our officers was seventy-two (72) and a large portion of them had never used a computer or even knew how to use a mouse. We decided to set up units for thirty (30) trainees at a time in the county's large multi-purpose room. My Assistant Registrar, Gary Talkington, and I were responsible for the training. This method was chosen because we had to do the training quickly due to an election quickly approaching and so that if there were questions everyone could hear the same answer.

When we finished the training, both Gary and I felt confident that the vast majority of trainees would perform confidently on Election Day. Well, we were wrong! When Election Day arrived four (4) of the twenty-four polling places could not open their pollbooks. While I was working with the chief officers of those precincts, two of my board members made a decision that would affect us not only that day but for months and years later. I will go into further detail on this a little later. From this you will see that no matter how hard you try there are some things you cannot foresee and are outside your control. There was a comment on Facebook recently that represents this: "Have you ever felt like you did everything right . . . and it still all went wrong?" And it did.

However, even with this incident, electronic pollbooks are much better for the officers of election and my staff. The pollbooks automatically gave the officers the number of voters for the Statement of Results and provided us the information we needed to give voter credit for those who participated in the election. This was done manually before and was very cumbersome. Electronic pollbooks were a great solution.

E-pollbooks – examples of new design

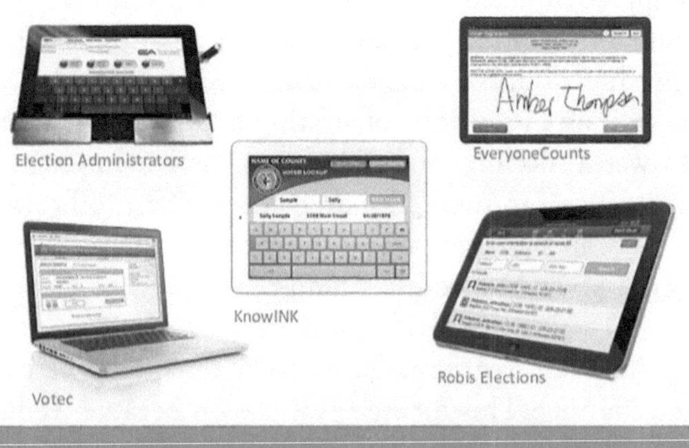

All of our machines were kept in a storage facility in another building within Christiansburg. Over the years we moved from the basement of the Government Center building, to a special storage area built to our specifications in an industrial park in Blacksburg, to the basement of an old library. Only the industrial park facility was sufficient for our needs. The last storage area was dusty, had a concrete floor, and the wiring was not sufficient for our needs. Zeke Bleakley and I put a rubber floor down to make it easier on our feet when we had to spend days at the storage area programming the voting machines or the pollbooks. This did help but we were forced to spend a lot of money over the years replacing UPS batteries because of the wiring and the heat in the storage area. We also experienced flooding issues when we had large rainstorms. I requested a different location, but it seemed to fall on deaf ears in County Administration. Then one day, after we had to replace several of the batteries in our laptops and UPS units, they gave us a new air conditioner that helped us. Hopefully my successor will be able to get this moved to a more appropriate area.

Hopefully you can see that to be a director of elections/general registrar, you have to be more than an office manager, you must be a technical wizard, human resource professional, trainer, budget manager, and event planner all wrapped up in one. In local government you must be versatile and willing to do what is needed.

One other thing I need to mention here is what we do for voters with disabilities. These voters didn't have many choices before the introduction of touchscreen machines. They either had to apply for an absentee ballot and have someone assist them at home, come to polls and have someone with them in the voting booth, or complete a paper ballot with someone's help. When the touchscreen machines became available they could be used by individuals with disabilities and they could vote like everyone else. This was a great move forward for a significant part of our population. I even got a call and an email from a professor at Radford University thanking me for introducing these new machines because she was able to vote like everyone else for the first time. She was blind and could use the earphones and follow the instructions of the recorded voice. Obviously, this had a very emotional effect on me. It was another valuable service we could provide.

When we went to the optical scan equipment, and ELECT said we could no longer use the WINvote machines touchscreen machines, we purchased the Unisyn OVI machines. We now have one of these machines at every precinct and this allows the disabled voter to vote like everyone else by printing out a paper ballot that can be read by the OVO scanner.

However, individuals with disabilities and voters over sixty-five (65) can also vote curbside if necessary. All they must do is notify the General Registrar's office what time they will be at the curbside spot, tell one of the party officials outside the polls or send someone in to the polling place and we will bring the ballot out to them. We generally send two officers of election outside to oversee the process (one from each party) but if they are slammed inside the chief officer could come out on his/her own. This process is used quite often and benefits a significant number of voters.

====================== **CHAPTER FIVE** ======================

The Virginia Election and Registration Information System (VERIS)

Now that you have been told about the electronic pollbooks, I need to mention how we got the information to populate them. When I first got into the business, the State Board of Elections (SBE) used a cobalt system that was very limited but we in the field had a lot of confidence in it because, as long as you put good information in, you knew that the reports and pollbooks you got out were correct. Unfortunately, the system was old and there were fewer and fewer people that knew the computer language to keep it operating.

When the Help America Vote Act (HAVA) was passed in 2002, SBE saw an opportunity to upgrade the Commonwealth's database system. There was federal money available and we needed a more robust system. Jean R. Jensen, Secretary of the State Board, developed a committee made up of computer experts and general registrars across the state. Their task was to determine the best course of action—develop your own system or purchase a system already developed for another state. After much study and evaluation, they chose to go with a system developed for Indiana. The drawback with this system was that it had to be modified to meet Virginia law and our needs. When SBE decided to roll the new database system out, they put a lot of effort into training everyone. They were faced with a monumental task because many of the GRs across the state were not computer literate. It took a lot of one-on-one training and then these individuals had to rely on their colleagues to help them when they got stuck. When this was rolled out I had two (2) employees who were experts in the old system but terrified of the new one. We had to go slow and constantly used the "Sandbox" which was a mirrored training system. After about six months hunting and pecking in the system, everyone in the office was proficient in VERIS.

Unfortunately, at the beginning SBE had difficulty in getting VERIS to work properly. We could never be sure that the information we were getting out was correct. We would be told to rerun reports or to enter information again. When they made a change to one process it would affect three others. This is not good when you have elections every year like Virginia. Everyone was concerned before an election if we would get all the information we needed for the pollbooks. Also, the system would go down periodically, and we could not enter information or would have to rely on our paper files to operate. The last thing we would want is for VERIS to go down on Election Day. We would lose our database and not be able to check where voters registered in other counties and cities should vote. In one instance before an election, VERIS was down for two weeks. No information was put in and no reports were run. Fortunately, SBE was able to get the system back up and running and everything went well. But what would happen if it didn't?

It took several years to stabilize the program and a lot of credit must go to Matthew Davis. When he first came aboard he was known as Nancy Rodrigues's friend. Ms. Rodrigues was the Secretary of the State Board and was appointed by Governor Tim Kaine. I will go into much greater detail later on Ms. Rodrigues's and Governor Kaine's effects on SBE's relations with the general registrars and the direction we were taken with Governor Kaine. Matt lived in the same neighborhood with Ms. Rodrigues and she hired him to help with VERIS. At first, he was as lost as the rest of us, but Matt took responsibility and ownership for the changes and eventually had a great team around him to get things under control. Matt deserves credit for the turnaround and getting VERIS to the point we were confident in how it operated. He also developed the photo ID software and software to easily run our pollbooks before each election. Matt always had a lot of patience and never seemed to let his emotions get too high or low in communicating with us. He was always in control. Just before I left, he was working on a software package for our poll-books that would be free to localities. I am sure he will be successful with this too.

"A million dollar system, and we forget to invest in a $40 surge protector!"

=========== **CHAPTER SIX** ===========

Voter Registration & Voter ID – Issues that should not be controversial but were!

For the first four (4) years of my tenure, voter registration was one of our easiest responsibilities. During this time voters were responsible for making sure they were registered to vote. They either came into our office to complete the Voter Registration Application or picked one up at the local post offices or public libraries and mailed them to us. Voters could also register to vote at the local Department of Motor Vehicles or the Department of Social Services. My predecessor also got approval from the Department of Justice for us to visit the county high schools to allow the seniors to register. This way we always had a constant flow of new voters (Montgomery County was constantly growing due to the growth of Virginia Tech) and hovered around 55,000–57,000 registered voters for our county prior to 2008. This made us confident with our numbers and that our voters did live within Montgomery County.

The 2008 Presidential Election turned our world upside down. The Barack Obama Campaign decided to concentrate on getting college students to vote where they were attending school instead of their family's home address. The Code of Virginia allowed the individual to determine what they considered their primary residence, and this opened the floodgates for those of us in college towns. On August 1 and the first week of October, we had over 8,000 new registrations. With a staff of four, we had to work nights and weekends throughout this time to get all of the new voters in the system. You must remember we had to also prepare for the election during this time. There was no rest for the weary. Thankfully we had other general registrars to assist us. Two of these great election officials were Dana Oliver of Salem City and Barbara Gunter of Bedford County. I will go into much more detail later about these outstanding officials when I talk about their commitment to the profession and their assistance to me over the years. Additionally, the State Board of Elections sent some staff members up to help. As a result, our voter numbers increased dramatically. Not only did this massive increase in voters affect us in the office, we had to prepare for a much larger flow of voters on Election Day. I will expand on this later and provide a better explanation for the "perfect storm" that occurred during this election. You will not believe what happened and the efforts we made to alleviate the massive turnout.

Unfortunately, these new voters not only created issues for us during the election, they also made it harder for us to be certain that all of our voters lived within Montgomery County or were US citizens and eligible to vote. Students at Virginia Tech normally only live on campus their freshman year. Unless they continue their education during the summer, they also go back home to be with their parents. The next three or four years they move around town from apartment to apartment. During this time, they fail to tell us that they have moved and, when and if they decide to vote again, they are in the wrong precinct. Additionally, when they graduate and leave our area, they are not thinking about voting and many times discover they have not changed their registration before it is too late to vote. We could not tell you for certain that every voter registered in Montgomery County lived here or that everyone was eligible to vote.

I mention the issue of legal residence and citizenship because it has always been a great concern of mine. When I first got into the election business, the State Electoral Board's (SBE) position on residence was much stricter than it is now. The registrant had to have proof of their permanent legal residence in order to register. In 2006–2007 there was a move to reduce these requirements because the Democratic controlled SBE and the Governor felt it was too much of a burden on the registrant. They felt the statement on the application form the applicant signed was sufficient since they acknowledged if they provided false information they would be subject to being charged with a felony. However, we have encountered many instances of fraud by applicants and have submitted them to our Commonwealth Attorney for action. They never move past the investigation part of the process because they are politicians too and must run for their positions every four years. They do not want to be seen going after voters, unless there is significant evidence like in Harrisonburg where an individual submitted numerous fake applications leading up to the 2016 Presidential Election. This individual left the area and was finally apprehended in Maryland. Additionally, the Department of Elections in their periodic check with the Department of Motor Vehicles, discovered several noncitizens who had registered and voted. We would be notified to take them off the rolls. This issue needs to be resolved or many voters will have the ability to vote in multiple states and noncitizens will be able to vote in elections in which they are not eligible. This will also be addressed later when I get into specifics. I had a specific situation where four (4) voters voted in Montgomery County and in Illinois during the 2012 Presidential Election. The Commonwealth Attorney's office and the Virginia State Police chose not to act against the people because they were living in Illinois and they said they didn't realize what they had done. You have got to be kidding me. They didn't know what they were doing? Of course, they knew what they were doing! If the authorities are not going to do anything with evidence like this, then they never will.

Voter ID is a political issue. Democrats and Republicans have polar opposite positions on it. The Democrats constantly side with not requiring ID while Republicans feel IDs are necessary to ensure the sanctity of voting. I could never understand why you would not want to confirm the voter's identity. When you do anything else in society you must show ID, so why wouldn't you do this with something as important as voting? The Democrats keep saying minorities and the elderly cannot get IDs, but the Virginia General Assembly took care of this by providing camera equipment for our office to provide free ID for people who did not have them. The vast majority of voters also already have the number one ID—Virginia Driver's License. This puts a hole in the theory that an ID is not easily accessible.

There is much, much more to voter registration than the public knows. One must remember voters move in and out of localities all the time and they do so even more in university/college counties. When someone registered in Tennessee decides to go to school at Virginia Tech and to register to vote here, we must notify the election officials in Tennessee about this move, so they can take the person off their rolls. One major issue with this is that we rely on the voter being honest and telling us he/she is registered in the other state. There have been several instances all across Virginia where voters attending colleges and universities have bragged to others that they have voted twice during Presidential Elections—here in Virginia and in their home state. Just like with illegals, if the voter is not honest and does not provide the correct information, we are at their mercy and fraud can be committed. Something more needs to be done to correct this. If the applicant lies on the form or does not provide us with the information needed, they are to be held responsible and must be held accountable in court. It should be automatic and not left up to Commonwealth Attorneys to decide if action should be taken. If they are found guilty they must be held accountable and pay the price. Our election system is sacred and must be protected. If nothing is done, some people will continue to commit fraud and one day an election will be determined by voters who are not eligible to vote. It may have already happened in the 2012 Presidential Election because a study was just done by Old Dominion University indicating that a huge number of illegals voted in this election.

The Department of Elections has the following information on their website:

About Virginia Voter Photo Identification

Virginia law requires all voters to provide an acceptable form of **photo identification** (photo ID) when voting in person at their polling place. There are many different types of photo IDs that a voter may use when they vote. All of the acceptable forms of photo ID can be used up to a year after ID has expired.

These photo IDs include:

- Valid Virginia Driver's License or Identification Card
- Valid Virginia DMV issued Veteran's ID card
- Valid United States Passport
- Other government-issued photo identification cards (must be issued by US Government, the Commonwealth of Virginia, or a political subdivision of the Commonwealth)
- Tribal enrollment or other tribal ID issued by one of 11 tribes recognized by the Commonwealth of Virginia
- Valid college or university student photo identification card (must be from an institution of higher education located in Virginia)
- Valid student ID issued by a public school or private school in Virginia displaying a photo
- Employee identification card containing a photograph of the voter and issued by an employer of the voter in the ordinary course of the employer's business

Virginia Department of Elections
Washington Building
1100 Bank Street, First Floor
Richmond, VA 23219

CHAPTER SEVEN

Keeping Voter Records & Placing the Voter in the Correct Precinct

I mentioned in "Chapter Four" the paper records we keep. They are the voter registration applications completed by the applicant. Prior to my last year of service, the application forms were designed so that they would fit in our specially designed file cabinets. Then someone in the Department of Elections decided to change the form without considering our input and completely changed the size of the form. We now had to go through several steps to make them fit in our file cabinets. This is the one thing that really gets under the skin of those of us in the field when the people in Richmond who have never worked out in the field make decisions without listening to us. It is another unfunded mandate from Richmond. They were passing the cost of business on to the localities again. Unfortunate!

This application provided the following information:

- Full Name
- Address
- Phone Number
- Social Security Number
- Sex
- Birth Date

- Acknowledgement that they are eligible to register to vote, age, not judged mentally incapacitated, a citizen, live within the jurisdiction where they are applying, etc.
- If already registered, the applicant is to tell us where, so we can cancel their registration at that locality

Virginia Voter Registration Application

Use blue or black ink

*Starred (*) items are required. If you do not complete all of the items that are marked with *, your application may be denied (See instructions on reverse side).*

1. ☐ YES ☐ NO — * I am a citizen of the United States of America. | * Full social security number ☐ No SSN was ever issued. | * Date of birth | * Gender

2.
* Last name __________ Jr. Sr. II III IV *(Circle if applicable)*
* First name __________ * Middle name __________ ☐ None
* Residence address *(May not be a P.O. Box)* __________ Apt # __________
* City/Town __________ * ZIP __________
E-mail __________ Phone __________

3. * Have you ever been convicted of a felony <u>or</u> judged mentally incapacitated and disqualified to vote? .... ☐ YES ☐ NO   If YES, has your right to vote been restored? ...... ☐ YES ☐ NO

4.
☐ I am an active-duty uniformed services member, spouse or dependent; or an overseas citizen.

☐ I am providing a mailing address *(below)* because my residence address is not serviced by the U.S. Postal Service <u>or</u> I am homeless.
▶ I am providing a <u>Virginia P.O. Box</u> *(below)* to protect my residence address from public disclosure because:

☐ I am an active <u>or</u> retired law enforcement officer, judge, U.S. or Virginia Attorney General attorney
☐ I have a court issued protective order for my benefit
☐ I have evidence of filing a complaint with law enforcement that either I <u>or</u> a household member is in fear for personal safety from another person who has threatened or stalked either me <u>or</u> a household member
☐ I am a participant in the Virginia Attorney General's Address Confidentiality Program

My mailing address *(Complete only if you have checked a box in this section)*

5. ☐ I am currently registered to vote in another state: ___ ___ . *(Indicate state of previous registration)*

6. ☐ I am interested in being an Officer of Election (poll worker) on Election Day. *Please send me information.*

7. AFFIRMATION: I swear/affirm, under felony penalty for making willfully false material statements or entries, that the information provided on this form is true. I authorize the cancellation of my current registration and I have read the Privacy Act Notice.

* Signature __________   Today's date: __________

☐ By checking this box, I affirm both that I am an individual with physical disabilities and the Affirmation Statement above. Pursuant to Article II, § 2 of the Constitution of Virginia, individuals with physical disabilities are not required to sign the application for voter registrations.

- ✂

*** Virginia Voter Registration Application Receipt**

The application collector must submit your completed application within 10 days or by the deadline to register for the next election, whichever comes first. You can check your voter registration status online at *elections.virginia.gov/register*. If you do not receive confirmation of your voter registration status within 30 days, contact your local voter registrar or the Virginia Department of Elections.

Name, phone and e-mail of office, group or individual receiving application

__________ Date application received

Thank you for applying to vote in Virginia!

VA-NVRA-1 04/16

Once this information is entered into VERIS, we can place the person in the correct precinct. We write this precinct on the application form and also indicate if they are within one of the two towns for town elections.

In Montgomery County, we fluctuated between 56,000 to 67,000 records in our files. They had to be kept in alphabetical order and that wasn't as easy as one would think because of the forms placed in the files daily for the transfers in and removing the ones who have transferred out. When the voter transfers out to a locality somewhere in Virginia, we would send our card to the new locality, so they would have the full record on the voter.

All of this is very time consuming and tedious. Just think how difficult this was when we got the 8,000 plus applications from Virginia Tech just before the 2008 Presidential Election. Not only is it difficult to get all of the applications into VERIS, we must also file them in our cabinets before the election. With only four full-time employees we had to rely on some temporary staff to get this done in a timely manner. I can't imagine the number of staff it would take to keep this up in Fairfax County that has approximately 750,000 registered voters. This magnitude of voters may explain their decision to scan the applications into VERIS. We chose not to scan ours because I did not feel comfortable with the Department of Elections's technology being stable enough to always be available. All we needed was to have the internet go down on Election Day and we would not have access to the information on our voters. When the officers of election would call in and indicate a voter was not in their pollbook, it was up to us to determine if they were registered and if so, where would they vote? It was vital for us to keep this hard copy of the application to verify this information. We must now add to the director of elections/general registrar's job responsibilities that of a librarian.

Now let's get into how we place the voter in the correct precinct. Every ten years the federal government completes a census to determine our population and where the population has shifted for representation purposes. The population numbers are divided into census blocks. The states and localities take this information and try to the best of their ability to put similar numbers in each district.

The General Assembly in Virginia makes sure that the House of Representatives, State Senate and House of Delegates members will represent similar numbers of population. The Board of Supervisors or City Councils must make sure their supervisor or council members also represent a similar number of citizens. These government entities use the census blocks and natural boundaries to determine the boundaries of each district. We then use this information to determine the correct district and polling place to place our voters. These districts can change if population grows or shrinks during the ten (10) year period. Sometimes localities' strategic plans for development can shift populations while others may change due to the growth or lack of growth of jobs. The population of Montgomery County has grown tremendously over the almost thirteen (13) years of my tenure due to the growth of Virginia Tech and companies utilizing the university and Tech's Corporate Research Center (CRC). We have grown so much that our population now exceeds that of Roanoke County. But with the help of the county's Geographic Information System (GIS) staff, Robert Pearsal and Michael Sutherland, we were able to make sure everyone is placed in the right place. Frankly, we couldn't have done it without their expertise and guidance. They are two extremely knowledgeable and professional gentlemen. They were always great to work with and always took great pride in their work. Montgomery County is very fortunate to have these valuable assets.

We take the information GIS and us have collected and place it into VERIS. When we enter the information provided to us by the voter on the Voter Registration Application into VERIS, we are provided their exact House of Representatives, State Senate, and House of Delegates districts. We also need to know if the voter lives within the towns or not for town elections. The GIS staff also provides this info to us. When a voter calls us, and asks where they go to vote, not only can we tell them that, but we can also tell them exactly which districts they are in.

A director of elections/general registrar must also be a data entry operator and understand redistricting. Are you seeing the pattern here? A director of elections/general registrar must be a jack of all trades. If you think all of this can be done within an eight (8) hour day or forty (40) hour week you are mistaken, especially as elections get closer and the elections get more and more important to the voters. Every election is important to us because we must prepare the same way for each one. As I mentioned with the voter registrations we do every four years, some elections put more pressure on us than others. With our training sessions, we must do them during the day and at night. This must all be done at the same time we are preparing for the upcoming election and along with our other daily duties.

Thankfully redistricting only comes around every ten years. It is a very labor-intensive project and affects a lot of voters, so we must be very precise and be willing to explain to the public why we did what we did. When redistricting in 2011 was done, it was done as well as it could be. Marty McMahon, County Attorney, was given the responsibility to head up the committee on redistricting including the GIS staff and me. We accomplished the objective of creating equal numbers in our supervisory districts. These changes also required we make one precinct very small; B-1 had 400 voters so that voters would not have to travel too far to get to their polling place. It also increased the number of voters in E-2, Long-Shop McCoy Fire Department (from 900 to 1,800) to a point we were concerned with the size of the meeting room we used in the building and the number of parking spots outside. Several voters were displaced and had to travel to a polling place much farther away. We spent a lot of time on the phone talking with unhappy voters. Even though we provided an in-depth explanation of the process and the requirements we were required to follow, they were not happy. Like I said, it is good that this process only takes place every ten (10) years. I am glad I will not have to go through another one. But please understand that I appreciated the process and the staff members I worked with during it.

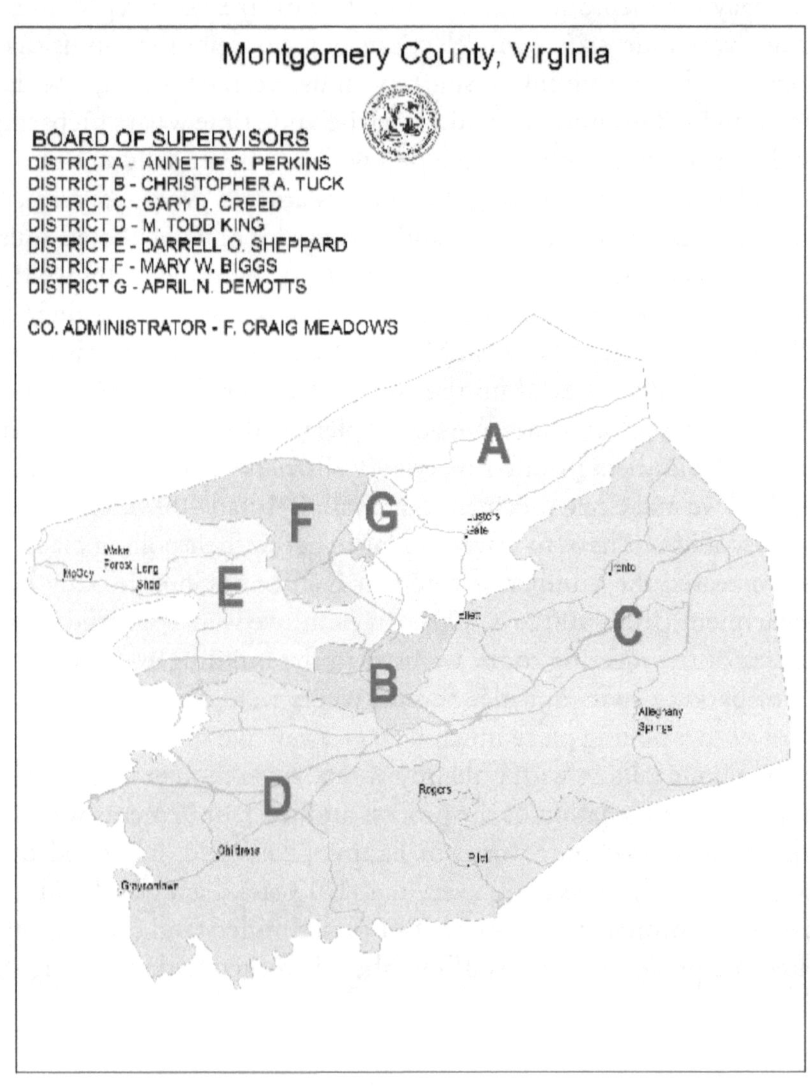
Montgomery County, Virginia
BOARD OF SUPERVISORS
DISTRICT A - ANNETTE S. PERKINS
DISTRICT B - CHRISTOPHER A. TUCK
DISTRICT C - GARY D. CREED
DISTRICT D - M. TODD KING
DISTRICT E - DARRELL O. SHEPPARD
DISTRICT F - MARY W. BIGGS
DISTRICT G - APRIL N. DEMOTTS
CO. ADMINISTRATOR - F. CRAIG MEADOWS
A
F
G
E
C
B
D

CHAPTER EIGHT

Candidate Processing and Campaign Finance

The Department of Elections has strict guidelines for being a candidate. They provide these guidelines on their website, *www.elections. virginia.gov*. What actions you take are determined by what position you are seeking and whether you are running as a Party candidate or an Independent. These guidelines also determine what and where you must file—either locally or through the Department of Elections. Now you would think that these guidelines are easy to understand and follow but most candidates need help in completing the forms and require assistance from our office. It is always a lot of fun working with the candidates because they generally have no idea what they are getting into. Not only will it be a challenge to win an election, the candidate requirements are very detailed and require a lot of time and effort to get through. I've had a couple of prospective candidates decide not to run because of the steps they had to take and the information you must share with the public. Not only do you have to share your personal information—address, phone number, and email address—you have to share your finances, and this is very difficult for many. Most candidates must also set up a separate bank account to place any political donations they may receive. Some however have decided not to take campaign donations and only use their finances to fuel their campaign and agree not to exceed $1,000 in total funds expended. By doing this, they do not have to submit

Campaign Finance Reports during the campaign. However, should they accept any donations or spend more than the $1,000, they must start providing the campaign finance reports at the next due date. I must also mention that they must keep detailed records of who made the donations and how much they received from each person. This information is provided in each Campaign Finance Report. Now we add the responsibility of guidance counselor to the long list of duties of the director of elections/general registrar.

Normally in order to have elections, you must have candidates. However, there are times no one wants to go through the candidate process and will run a write-in campaign. This happened twice in my tenure for the District C School Board seat. Both times the candidates went out and purchased signs to post throughout their district informing the public they were running as a write-in candidate. They also complied with my request for them to complete a Declaration of Candidacy form, so we would know their correct name. The ballot has no candidates listed and only a space for a write-in candidate. We notified all of our officers of election in District C the names of the candidates running write-in campaigns, so they would know the correct names to look for on the ballot. One of these elections was held on the touchscreen voting machines and the other on our optical scan machines. Both elections took our officers quite a while to determine the winners. The optical scan machines actually were harder for the officers because they had to read the voters' handwriting to determine whom they had voted for. With handwriting as it is today, you can only imagine their difficulty.

There are those who want to run for a position with their political party's support. Sometimes these candidates are more difficult to work with than the independents because they must get the party's endorsement. Generally, this is done with a Mass Meeting or a Firehouse Primary. The Mass Meeting is simply when the party's membership gets together in one large meeting and after the candidates explain why they should be chosen and those in attendance vote. The candidate with the most votes gets the endorsement. It is imperative that the candidate get as many supporters as possible to the meeting. Some have even used buses to get their people there.

This is a very stressful process for the candidate and some have won by as few as one vote. Once they have received the endorsement, they know they have a large block of votes because a large number of voters simply vote by party—especially today with politics being so partisan.

The next option is a Firehouse Primary. With this option the party will create a ballot listing all the candidates and give all of the party's members a date and number of hours to be able to cast their ballot. They are generally held on a Saturday and the hours can fluctuate but have gone from 8:00 a.m. until 7:00 p.m. A committee is formed to count the votes and announce the winners. Both require that the candidate get as many people as possible to show up and vote for them, but this one doesn't require that the party member be in one place for a long period of time. They can choose when they want to stop by and vote.

Once the candidates have been chosen, the party chairperson completes specific paperwork received from the Department of Elections and returns it to them and provides a copy to our office. This way ELECT and we know who to place on the ballot with the party's endorsement. Once these names have been received, we can start working with the people who create our ballots. In our case, we utilized Election Services Online (ESO) who also programmed our voting machines. ESO had a challenge in producing our ballots because we had a large number of ballot styles. We had more than one of the most populous counties in the Commonwealth—Chesterfield County. I will go into more detail on this in a later chapter.

As previously mentioned, campaign finance is a very difficult process for the candidate and our office. The cover sheet and dates for their reports in 2017 is below:

· VIRGINIA ·
DEPARTMENT
of ELECTIONS

Campaign Committee
Campaign Finance Report
2017

Form
CFDA-947.4CS

Amendments	
☐ This is an amendment to a previously filed report.	Amendment #

Committee Information

Committee Name	Committee ID #
Mailing Address (include city, state, and zip)	Date of Election M/D/Y
	Office Sought
	Locality/District

For official use only

Preparer Information

Email Address	Daytime Telephone #

Report Date

Check one square below

May Election	November Election	Special Election	Non-Election Year
Candidates in this year's May general election have reports due on the following dates:	Candidates in this year's June primary and/or November general election have reports due on the following dates:	Candidates in any election this year not taking place on the day of a general election have reports due on the following dates:	Candidates who are not up for election in 2017 have reports due on the following dates:
☐ February 27, 2017*	☐ April 17, 2017	☐ Pre-election (8 days before the election)	☐ July 17, 2017
☐ April 17, 2017	☐ June 5, 2017		☐ January 16, 2018
☐ April 24, 2017	☐ July 17, 2017		
☐ June 15, 2017	☐ September 15, 2017	☐ Post-election (30 days after the election or prior to taking office, whichever is sooner)	
☐ July 17, 2017	☐ October 16, 2017		
☐ January 16, 2018	☐ October 30, 2017		
	☐ December 7, 2017		
*For candidates participating in a March primary only.	☐ January 16, 2018		

No Activity Statement

☐ I declare, subject to felony penalties pursuant to the Code of Virginia § 24.2-1016, that except for the addition of interest or dividend payments and/or subtraction of any bank service charges, no monies or other things of value have been received and no monies have been expended for this reporting cycle; any interest or dividend payments and/or subtraction of bank service charges will be reported on the appropriate schedule of the next report for any period in which other activity occurs. The balance on hand at the end of the last reporting period with activity was:

$ _______________

Statement of Treasurer or Custodian of the Books

☐ I declare, subject to felony penalties pursuant to the Code of Virginia § 24.2-1016, that this report for the period M/D/Y through M/D/Y , including all accompanying schedules, is to the best of my knowledge true, correct, and complete.

M / D / Y

Signature of Treasurer or Custodian of the Books   Date

Revised: 12/15/2016

As you can see from the dates listed in 2017, there are many and they get closer together as we get closer to Election Day. The candidate is responsible for providing this report by end of the day on the dates listed. The candidate has the right to file either by paper or by computer. ELECT developed a software package for campaign finance called COMET. They encourage the candidates to use this software and quite frankly it is much better for them. The software is intuitive, and when the candidate lists one contribution the software leads them to the next appropriate question. The candidate does not have to guess where to go on the report. The feedback I got from candidates was always very positive.

Once the report has been filed, it is the responsibility of the general registrar/director of elections to review the report and communicate with the candidate if there is something in the report that does not make sense and needs to be corrected. This was the responsibility of the Secretary of the Electoral Board but was changed a couple of years ago. It is now the responsibility of the GR to confirm that the report has been filed in a timely manner and appears to be completed correctly. If the report is not filed in a timely manner, the Code of Virginia is very clear that the candidate will be fined. If the candidate does not file the report within a defined time period, the fine gets larger. The fines can get pretty large for local candidates. Statewide candidates do receive larger contributions and handle these fines much better. Local candidates, however, are hit harder. The fines must be paid to the County Treasurer and placed in the General Fund for the locality. I believe the money should go back into elections because they are becoming more and more expensive.

I would like to describe a situation that happened a few years back during the Commonwealth Attorney's race regarding a campaign finance issue. After the Fourth of July parade, the Democratic candidate Dennis Nagel came into my office and lodged a complaint saying his opponent, Republican candidate Brad Finch, had not listed expenditure for T-shirts worn in the parade. I quickly checked Mr. Finch's last report and no expenditure for T-shirts was listed. I told him that the Electoral Board would have to hear his complaint at their next meeting. I notified the Board Secretary and a meeting was scheduled. Mr. Nagel presented his case and the board chose to proceed with the investigation. They got in touch with Mr. Finch and asked why the expenditure was not listed. Mr. Finch explained it very well. It turns out that he had not received the bill for the T-shirts and was going to list it on his next report that was due soon. This was a justifiable action since he did not know what the final expenditure was until he received the bill. Mr. Nagel's concern was justified, and Mr. Finch's explanation was also acceptable.

A couple of years ago the campaign finance responsibilities were transferred to the General Registrar when the job title was changed to Director of Elections. We must also be referees in this arena too.

═══════ CHAPTER NINE ═══════

VRAV and VEBA

The Voter Registrars Association of Virginia (VRAV) and the Virginia Electoral Board Association (VEBA) are the professional organizations that represent us. There can be as many as 133 regular members in VRAV because there are 133 cities and counties in Virginia. VEBA can have as many as 399 members since there are three (3) members of each board. This organization works very hard to educate legislators and the public on what we do and how we do it. When I first became a GR, many of the members of VEBA across the Commonwealth did not have the skills to perform their duties. They were told before assuming their positions that they would not have to do anything because the GR would handle everything. They would just have to attend a few meetings and get paid a monthly stipend. As elections have changed and more technical knowledge is needed, many have left or been replaced. The VEBA members today are knowledgeable of technology and all aspects of the voting machines and electronic pollbooks. They are also becoming more involved in the daily operation. It is imperative that all GRs keep their board members informed of what is going on and issues that arise.

During the thirteen (13) years as a member of VRAV, I was fortunate to serve as the president and part of the executive committee for a four (4) year period. I learned quite a lot during this time and became very familiar with the intricacies of the organization. It also made it possible for me to get to know most of its members very well. I was also able to get to know a good number of VEBA members over the years. The VEBA members I got to know well from other localities were all very professional and serious about their responsibilities. I keep in touch today with many of them.

As in any organization, there are those who seek power and are only concerned with increasing their stature within the group. These individuals would go to great lengths to create dissension. As in all professional organizations, VRAV had bylaws but many of these troublemakers constantly tried to go around them to achieve their goals. They would also condemn those of us who followed the bylaws and recommended they do the same. I understand from a recent conversation that they have finally followed the process and have gotten their recommendations for future elections approved. There can be multiple candidates for each position. Once this process is changed, they will hopefully be satisfied, but I don't believe so. Some people just can't stay away from controversy.

There have always been two distinct factions within VRAV. There is the Eastern faction and the Western faction. The Eastern faction is made up of those localities east (Richmond and Tidewater) and north (NOVA) of Charlottesville and the Western faction includes those localities to the west of Charlottesville. The ones to the east are generally larger in population, have more staff, and conduct business differently because of it. In my opinion they forget the localities to the west that have less wealth and a much smaller tax base and have much less staff to conduct the same processes. I grew up in a small town in Southwest Virginia and understood the difficulties these professionals experienced on a daily basis, so I fought for them. I believe I won the election for president because of my support of the smaller localities and from growing up in one of those small localities (Smyth County). There is a different mentality in those on the East Coast and in Northern Virginia. This is also prevalent in the Virginia General Assembly. The senators and delegates tend to also forget the localities west of Charlottesville. Less funding and programs come this way because of the lack of representation in the General Assembly—again due to lack of population. But I digress from the two organizations representing the election officials in Virginia.

Let me get back to VRAV. When I went to my first VRAV meeting I was taken aback with the lack of cohesiveness within the organization. There was a lot of bickering over the issues affecting us all. There were definite leaders in the two groups. One of these leaders was contrary to what I have said about the makeup of the two groups. He was the director of elections/general registrar for Chesterfield County—one of the largest counties in population in the Commonwealth, and he represented everyone in the organization—both large and small. His name is Lawrence "Larry" Haake. My first exposure to Larry really came during this first meeting. The Eastern Group was presenting their dissatisfaction with something the executive committee was doing. Then a very tall gentleman stood up and started speaking with a very deep voice. His voice and manner of speaking got your attention immediately. All eyes and ears came to attention and focused on Larry. Then he began his explanation as to why their complaint was not unfounded. He did it in a very logical manner and used the exact words from the bylaws. He won the argument and my respect. He was a true leader, and during my tenure in Montgomery County, he was elected our association president twice. Larry is a true Southern Gentleman and represented our organization in the highest manner. He intimidated me at the beginning, but it wasn't long before we became the best of friends. I have been blessed by knowing him and will go into further detail on Larry's contributions when I cover the interactions with the Virginia Department of Elections/SBE and the infamous Secretary of State Board, Nancy Rodrigues. Some other VRAV presidents who had a positive influence and made great contributions to promoting professionalism were Barbara Gunter, Bedford County; Lisa Jeffers, Waynesboro City; and Tracy Howard, Radford City. These two ladies and gentleman did a lot to bring the Department of Elections, VRAV, and VEBA together. Barbara, in my opinion, was and is the wisest of all of us. She has always had the ability to process incoming information at a high rate of speed and respond in the most professional manner at all times. Barbara can listen to a person's rant, process the pros and cons, refute everything the person has said using logic and facts, and make the person feel good about being corrected. Whenever I needed some input on a vital issue, I knew I would get an honest and straightforward response. She is a true jewel in a very hostile and combative environment.

Lisa Jeffers is another hard worker and has the ability to get people to work together on the hardest of projects. Her personality is radiant, and she can make you feel at ease in any situation. Lisa continued the fight to bring our salaries up to par to others with our responsibilities, e.g., Commissioners of Revenue and Treasurers. Unfortunately, we did not have the political power to get any movement on this.

I would be remiss if I didn't mention one of the real leaders within VEBA. The person who constantly works to further the goals of VEBA is Robin Lind (Goochland County). Robin is a true gentleman and his English accent provides him a distinct advantage when engaging in debates and in public speaking. He, like Barbara Gunter, has a presence about him that demands your attention. Robin may be one of the best orators I have ever seen. He is now the president of VEBA. His work behind the scenes is immeasurable. He does the VEBA newsletter and he spends almost every day at the Virginia General Assembly working on behalf of VEBA and VRAV. Yes, he worked on our behalf too because he had a comprehensive knowledge of what we did, and he also felt we were being taken advantage of.

Two other champions for VEBA are Renee Andrews (Falls Church City) and Bill Bell (Isle of Wight County). They work tirelessly for the organization and also on the behalf of general registrars all across the Commonwealth. We appreciated their efforts on our behalf.

VRAV and VEBA have continued their efforts on our behalf with a joint committee—the GREB Workgroup. Obviously, the GR stands for general registrar and the EB stands for the electoral board. This committee's first meeting was on September 4, 2014. Edgardo Cortes would have been the Commissioner of the Department of Elections. The original members were cochairs John Hager and Jean

Jensen. EB members were Bill Bell, Renee Andrews, Tommy Doxey, and Robin Lind. The GR members were Larry Haake, Tracy Howard, and Barbara Gunter. Martha Brissette from ELECT (Department of Elections) was assigned to assist the committee. This great group of leaders has worked very hard to define what general registrars/directors of elections do and show that we are as the title of the book says, *Overworked and Underpaid*. They have completed salary and staffing studies to present to the member of the General Assembly. Hopefully sometime in the future the General Assembly will recognize the contributions of this group of 133 professionals.

Virginia Electoral Board Association—representing more than 5,000,000 registered voters across the Commonwealth of Virginia

CHAPTER TEN

The Virginia State Board of Elections/ Department of Elections

Christopher Piper, Commissioner of Elections (2018)

I have waited until this point to provide information on the Department of Elections because you needed to know what we did before I mention how they affect our daily operations. Plus, it is not always a positive influence. When I first became a general registrar, the Department of Elections was called the State Board of Elections (SBE). The actual board was made up of three members: the chairman, vice chairman, and secretary. All members of the board were appointed by the governor. The board included two members from the governor's party and one from the other. The Secretary of the State Board (Jean Jensen) was also responsible for the staff of the State Board and received a full-time salary. The other members of the board were not paid. They didn't even receive mileage for their efforts and that didn't make any sense because these individuals spend a lot of time and put a lot of effort into their responsibilities.

There were about thirty-five (35) staff members and they were responsible for campaign finance, elections, law issues and guidance, training, and computer systems. There was also a deputy secretary position that assisted the secretary in whatever was necessary. This position generally did special projects and filled in when the secretary was not available. There was a director for each of the areas mentioned earlier. This entity was formed to ensure uniformity in elections throughout Virginia. As I mentioned earlier this is very difficult because of the differences in the sizes of staff. SBE would make interpretations of the Code of Virginia and then provide guidelines for the GRs. It was then the general registrar's and electoral board's responsibilities to make sure the processes were implemented.

The first secretary I dealt with was Ms. Jean Jensen. She was from Northern Virginia and had been very active in the Democrat Party. Jean, in my opinion, represented the very best in leadership. Although she was representing the Democrat Party, she always made decisions based on what was best for the voters and elections in general. She caught a lot of grief from other members of her party because of this. Those of us in the business appreciated her approach.

When I became the general registrar, I was faced with having to decide on what voting machines to purchase. The Help America Vote Act (HAVA) came about because of the fiasco in Florida after the 2000 Presidential Election. Congress didn't want the hanging chads to happen again, so they passed the law to replace all of the lever and punch card voting machines. They also added federal money to the pot to help pay for the new machines. Our lever machines were being held together with chewing gum and rubber bands (just kidding) and we needed new machines.

At this time the SBE had approved six (6) different vendors and all of them had touch screen machines. There was a group within the Blacksburg area, which included the League of Women Voters, that did not want us to switch to these machines. This group included the Chairman of the Democrat Party, Steve Cochran. Their opposition was based on the machines being electronic and they felt they could easily be tampered with.

The League of Women Voters called for a forum on the machines. The panel was made up of House of Delegates members Jim Shuler (D) and Dave Nutter (R) who were both against the machines; Dean Dowdy, Montgomery County Electoral Board Secretary and I represented the board and were obviously for the new machines. Knowing we were at a distinct disadvantage with the pending large crowd, I contacted Ms. Jean Jensen, SBE Secretary, and asked her to be on the panel. Ms. Jensen drove to Christiansburg from Richmond on the afternoon of the forum. This turned out to be a very smart move and helped our cause. Ms. Jensen not only held her own against the delegates but her presence and ability to explain clearly why we had to move forward turned many in our favor. I believe her presence at the forum helped clear the way for us to get the new machines and I will forever be indebted to her for making the trip and supporting us. As I have mentioned about Ms. Jensen, she always did what was best for the voter and the citizens of the Commonwealth even when her Democratic Party cohorts felt she didn't do enough for their advantage. She was a true example of what a secretary of the State Board of Elections should be.

When a new governor was elected (Tim Kaine), we knew that a new secretary would be appointed. We had heard that Ms. Nancy Rodrigues had received the appointment and I got to meet the new secretary at the VRAV annual meeting where I was just elected VRAV president. She was very pleasant and said she looked forward to working with me. Little did I know that our relationship would later deteriorate to the point that I had to inform the membership of VRAV that the secretary of the State Board had lied to me and had plans to center more power in SBE. Her ultimate goal was to have all general registrars report directly to the secretary. VRAV was against any move like this and her action created even more distrust between us.

Ms. Rodrigues and I started out on very good terms. She recommended that the three organizations (SBE, VEBA, and VRAV) would have a conference call each week to discuss any issues important to us. We spoke every Tuesday at 9:00 a.m. We discussed strategies to improve our/GR's standing with the General Assembly since they determine our salaries, how to work together better, and morale, and how to deal with legislation being submitted while the General Assembly was in session. The VEBA President was Maggie Luca from Fairfax County. Maggie was a real professional and fought very hard for VEBA and her political beliefs. Remember since the Governor was a Democrat, the Secretary was a Democrat, and since Maggie was the Secretary of the Fairfax County Board she was a Democrat. So, the Democratic position on many items including student registrations was going to be promoted in our meetings. This issue will become a major factor in my confrontation with the Obama Campaign and the "Drive-By" news media in 2008. This episode in my life will be explained in a later chapter.

The State Board of Elections/Department of Elections has/had many dedicated employees. Without these staff members SBE/ELECT would have failed and not accomplished many of its goals. One of these brave souls was Matthew Able. Matt is no longer with the Department of Elections and is working in Chesterfield County. While at SBE/ELECT, he was the most dedicated and knowledgeable person there. He cared about us across Virginia and would do whatever was needed to make sure we were successful. Matt worked fifty-six to sixty hours a week for several months prior to each election. Even when we messed up on something, e.g., abstracts, VERIS reporting, etc., he would call and lead you through what was needed. He did it without making you feel stupid or uncomfortable. You felt sorry that you had let him down in not getting it right. He is a true gentleman and someone we all (VRAV) trusted. Unfortunately, the Secretaries and Commissioner of Elections did not recognize or compensate him for his efforts. Larry Haake, the General registrar in Chesterfield, however, was happy to have him as a member of his staff. Matt's contributions to VRAV can never be repaid. We are just happy he is still part of us.

There are several other people I must mention who were available to us and helped us get our jobs done: Garry Ellis is responsible for registrations, felons, etc. Garry was also a great golf buddy. Our business is very stressful, and Garry brought a little humor to us all. I am appreciative of his assistance, guidance, and sense of humor. Susan Lee was responsible for training and uniformity and had a very difficult job. As mentioned, our jurisdictions come with various populations and staff. Trying to make sure everyone is doing everything the same is almost impossible, but Susan did it with the right frame of mind. Chris Piper was responsible for campaign finance. No one, and I mean no one, knew campaign finance better than Chris. I really enjoyed his attempt at making our annual meetings interesting. It was always a futile effort, but he was worth the price of admission. They have made considerable contributions to SBE/ELECT and to us in the field. They needed to be recognized for their service to the voters in Virginia and to VRAV.

CHAPTER ELEVEN

Dealing with the Public

Election officials strive very hard to build the public's trust. Those that are truly doing their jobs are nonpolitical. We must treat every applicant, candidate, and voter equally and with the same enthusiasm. I was fortunate to have been told by one Party Chairman's wife (who was an attorney) that I had met that goal. This meant a lot to me since her husband had wanted another applicant in my position and had pressured the two board members of his party to select someone else. Her words and how she said them got me through many rough days.

Dealing with the public is the most difficult job in the world. No matter what you do, you cannot make everyone happy. As I have mentioned, we are required by law to uphold Section 24.2 of the Code of Virginia. Unfortunately, the public doesn't care. They always want us to make exceptions because their circumstances are different. Let me go over a few circumstances all GRs have encountered:

- I heard from one GR who had been cursed last week for not being able to send someone an absentee ballot. By law the last date for us to send a ballot by mail is 5:00 p.m. on the Tuesday before the election. The person called on Wednesday and was told he would have to come into the office to vote in-person absentee or go to the polls. He cursed her and said she was trying to keep him from voting. We start sending out absentee ballot requests forty-five (45) days prior to the election, so he had plenty of time to get his application in and waited until it was too late. It turned out the voter wanted to do absentee because he didn't get off his regular work day until 5:00 p.m. The polls don't close until 7:00 p.m. so he had two hours to get to his polling place. He just didn't want to be inconvenienced. In today's world, voters do not want to be inconvenienced. They want us to go against the Code of Virginia to make their lives a little easier. Don't forget he had forty-five (45) days before the election to request his absentee ballot. The GR in this instance should not have been abused like this but we have all experienced it.

- Why do so many people procrastinate in voting absentee? In Virginia, absentee voting begins forty-five (45) days before the election. On the Absentee Ballot Application there are twenty reasons someone can vote absentee. But the vast majority will utilize Code 1D–Personal business or vacation outside County/City of residence on Election Day. You must also list the location where you are traveling. You would not believe the number of voters that list Roanoke, Salem, Radford, Floyd County, Pulaski County, and Giles County. Of course, these localities are adjacent to Montgomery County. In other words, they did not want to go to the polls on Election Day and wait in line. After the 2008 Presidential Election and the long lines we experienced, one of the political parties told its members to vote absentee to avoid the lines in the future. So, we would see the same people every election going out of the county. Fortunately, sometimes voters would come in and read the reasons for voting absentee and admit there wasn't a reason they could truthfully use and would leave without voting absentee. They simply said they could not lie. So, there are some people in this world who have morals.
- In Montgomery County we experience something very few localities across Virginia do. We have students from

Virginia Tech who have no idea about election laws and will try to get around them when they have no other option. For example, in Virginia a voter must vote at the polling place where they are registered. Obviously, many of the students at Tech are from other counties and towns around Virginia, from other states, or from outside the country. When they do not make arrangements to vote by absentee, they will show up either in our office or at the polls wanting to vote there. Even when we inform them they cannot vote with us, they get upset and take it out on the officers of election working the polls. This experience is very traumatic to the officers but it happens about every election. Even when the student knows they are registered somewhere else, they demand voting with us. We are required by law to provide the voter who thinks they should be registered in that precinct a provisional ballot. This ballot is a regular ballot that everyone else receives but is placed in a separate envelope and will be provided to the electoral board during the canvass (verifying of the election results). The general registrar will do research on the circumstances surrounding the provisional ballot and provide the information to the electoral board to make the determination if the ballot will be counted. Very few provisional ballots are counted because the voter is registered somewhere else or not registered at all. But there are times there has been a mistake either by another locality, the DMV, or even in our office, and the voter should have been placed in this precinct, and the electoral board will count the ballot. The general registrar is under a lot of pressure the morning after the election to gather as much information as he/she can get on each case. In a Presidential Election we would have as many as 75–125 provisional ballots and the electoral board would generally start the canvass at 1:00 p.m. This is another stressful time for general registrars. There is no rest for the weary!

- In Virginia a voter must have a physical address and cannot use a post office box or temporary mail box in a UPS store. We need a physical address in order to place the voter in the correct precinct. We received a voter registration application one day from a female (I can't say lady because of the names she called me) whose address was a PO Box in the UPS store in Blacksburg. I had to write a letter informing her I could not register her because of this. A few days later she came into the office threatening me and cursing up a storm. I tried to explain to her why I could not accept that address, but she would not stop yelling long enough for me to finish. Finally, she got tired and slowed down. I got some words in edgewise and she finally said she was homeless and living in her camper. Knowing the exact circumstances, I asked her if she attended a church in the area or knew someone that would receive her mail. She said she attended one of the churches in Blacksburg, so we got in touch with the minister and asked if he would accept her mail at that address. He said he would and our problem was solved. She used the church's address and she became a registered voter in Montgomery County.

- One of the areas where we as election officials always have confrontations with the public/political parties is outside the polls. Almost every election we have some people representing the parties/candidates handing out sample ballots or brochures to voters as they enter the polls. More often than not we have to have the chief officers go outside and ask these people to move back beyond the forty-foot limit by law. Some listen and adhere to the law but many will give the chief problems and I have to send the sheriff deputy assigned to us out to make it happen. The Deputy has on a few occasions had to threaten the person with arrest to get them to comply.

- I want to lump the news media in this section because they always say they are representing the public. Between you and me, the news media is as politically motivated as any individual and don't let them tell you otherwise. Instead of the media just providing you the facts like they did when I grew up, they must tell you how to interpret the information because you aren't smart enough to decide on your own. Like the "elite" politicians, the "elite" fourth estate think they are smarter than anyone and they will tell you so—especially the writers of the editorial section of the newspaper. *Wikipedia* defines the fourth estate (or fourth power) as a societal or political force or institution whose influence is not consistently or officially recognized. "Fourth Estate" most commonly refers to the news media, especially print journalism or "the press." In our area the *Roanoke Times* is that entity. You would think that this paper sitting in the middle of the conservative part of Virginia would reflect that in their writing. Not so much! The *Roanoke Times* is as liberal as they come. They praise every Democrat and cut down every Republican. Their editorials are always telling you how you should think and if you have conservative beliefs you are a threat to the very fiber of democracy. They wonder why they keep losing subscribers. Well it doesn't take an Einstein to figure it out. It would be so nice to go back when Walter Cronkite, Chet Huntley, and David Brinkley provided the news. They were all liberals, but they did not push their views on you. They just told you the facts and let you make the decisions. Today however, all of the news media especially ABC, CBS, and the ultra-liberal NBC (Nothing But Clinton) must guide you in their news stories. What is so funny about this is if the country became socialist like they want, they would not be able to say what they wanted. They would only be able to give the government's position on everything. They should be thankful for their freedom and want to be independent. It just shows you just how smart they really are!

- We have had about every primary election a voter or couple who see our voter signs out in front of the precincts and come into vote. They have no idea what the election is for or about but say they are there to vote. Some even show up at the wrong polling place and indicate their polling place was not open. Then we tell them that this election does not affect their district and they can't understand it. When one of the Parties has a Primary, we also have voters show up who vote in that polling place but when they discover it is a Democratic Primary, they say they would never vote in a Democratic Primary. It happens with the other Party too!

- The real kicker in dealing with the public is when you catch them doing something illegal, provide the judicial system evidence of a crime, and nothing is done. I was contacted by the registrar in Cook County, Illinois with a list of four names of voters who had voted in their Presidential Election and he thought they may have voted in the same election with us. After checking our records, all four had voted with us too. Here was the perfect example of voters breaking the law by voting twice. When I turned this information over to the Commonwealth Attorney's Office, she said she would look into it and get back to me. A week or two later I was contacted by the Assistant Commonwealth's Attorney and he arranged a meeting. We met in my office and he decided to bring in the state police, so they can work with the Illinois State Police. So, we met a couple of weeks later and the state police person said they would try to get in touch with the Illinois State Police and get them to talk with the voters who were living there now. Several weeks later, I received a call from the Assistant Commonwealth's Attorney saying they had researched the situation and spoken with the voters. He said after speaking with them they didn't feel the voters knew what they were doing. They said they didn't know it was illegal and they were doing anything wrong. So, he didn't think we should take this any farther and the matter was dropped. If law enforcement and the judicial system did not want to take this situation, where we had the facts to back it up, any further, then when would they? So, if anyone asks you if there is voting fraud, you can provide them this situation and say there certainly is.

Anyone who says, "the public is always right" has never worked with them.

CHAPTER TWELVE

The Bad Experiences and Dealing with Fake News!

❖ The 2008 Presidential Election – Registrations and Election Day

• The 2008 Presidential Election was unique for a couple of reasons. We had the first African-American candidate, Barack Hussein Obama, II, and had the largest turnout of college/university students. I was prepared for the much, much larger turnout because the media buzz leading up to the Presidential Primary was constant. To ensure we had enough ballots I ordered a ballot for each registered voter in each precinct. I rounded up with each of these numbers, so I was assured of having 100 percent of the ballots needed—this included any spoiled ballots. During the Presidential Primary, one county (Chesterfield County) didn't distribute their ballots adequately between polling places and a few ran out of ballots. They got emergency permission from the State Board of Elections to send out more ballots to these precincts, but the delay caused several voters to vote on handmade ballots and leave before they voted. The General Registrar was crucified by the news media, the Obama Campaign and the Democratic Party. The State Board of Elections (including the infamous Secretary–Nancy Rodrigues) did a review of what happened during the Primary and brought the General Registrar (Larry Haake) and his electoral board in to answer for this mistake. The hearing was brutal and as you will see in my situation in front of this same board there was a large turnout of GRs from across the Commonwealth to provide support for the GR because these circumstances were completely out of the ordinary. The public and the Parties have no idea of what we do or why we do it. But they will crucify you if something goes wrong.

I was prepared with ballots for the turnout in both the Primary and the General Election. But I was not ready for the number of student registrations and the precinct where they were placed. Let me explain. In previous General Elections the number of student registrations was negligible. But the Obama Campaign made student registrations at their college or university addresses a priority and they sent the Democratic Party; Move On.Org, a group out of Chicago; and Rock the Vote to Virginia Tech to get as many students as possible registered in Montgomery County. These groups set up tables all over the Virginia Tech campus and started getting students to complete the voter registration forms. This had not happened before, so we were not ready for the magnitude of registrations.

Between the middle of August until the second week of October we received well over 8,000 registration forms. Since there was only four of us in the office, that meant we each had 2,000+ registrations to research and enter into the VERIS database. We had to do this while we were programming voting machines and preparing for the election. This magnitude of registrations required my staff and I to work nights and weekends to get this done. We were fortunate to have Dana Oliver, City of Salem GR and Barbara Gunter, Bedford County GR, take time out of their busy schedule to come by and help us. We would do the in-person absentee voting and filing of applications during the day and entering the registrations during the evenings. Even with us working this hard, I was pushed off of VERIS by Ms. Rodrigues with thirty-five applications still not entered. This required me to write in the names and addresses of these voters in our pollbooks, so they could vote.

I need to mention here that the professors at Virginia Tech, who I believe are primarily democratic, invited these out of state organizations into their classrooms and helped put pressure on the students to register here in Montgomery County. These groups and some of the professors were not truthful with the students by telling them they could vote both here and their home states, and that it would be easier to vote here than at home. How do I know this? It is easy, once the students started thinking about what they had done, or their parents found out they had registered with us, they called us and asked that their registration be withdrawn. We had to tell them that we could only undo their application if we received a written notice from them with their signature stating they wanted to be removed from our rolls. We heard the stories from the students and received in writing numerous notes and letters asking to be removed. We also caught a student who had already voted in Tennessee and had registered to vote with us. When she realized she would be committing a felony if she voted with us, she wrote us a letter asking to have her registration withdrawn. So, these students doubled our work because we put them on our rolls and then had to take them off.

Now this deluge of voters, the vast majority from Virginia Tech, had placed them into one of our precincts—E1, St. Michael's Lutheran Church. Before this happened, St. Michael's had a little over 1,500 voters on its list of voters. After all these new voters were added they exceeded 6,000. The maximum number of voters in any one precinct by Code is 5,000 and that put us considerably over this amount. Unfortunately, in order to move a polling place, we have to go through a list of procedures including public hearings and this takes a minimum of two months. With the registrations ending the second week on October we did not have enough time to move it. We would also have to notify all voters in this precinct by mail that the polling place had been moved. We didn't have enough time for this either. So, we were stuck with trying to get all these voters into a small church on a two-lane road a couple of miles off of campus. We sent out press releases and arranged for the Montgomery County Public Schools to provide us a bus to transfer students who were driving their cars from a park and ride to vote. We also arranged for Blacksburg Transit to have several buses pick up students on campus to transport them to the polling place. Unfortunately, the vast majority of students decided to drive to this polling place. This created havoc on Election Day, especially after 4:00 p.m. when the students got out of class. Additionally, Rock the Vote brought their bus to this polling place. All of this created the "perfect storm." Too many cars and buses in a small parking lot and two-lane road created a traffic jam. The Sheriff's Office and the Virginia Department of Transportation tried to help us, but it was impossible to eliminate the congestion.

The bottomline was there was no way to prepare for this and you can only imagine the bad press we got.

Obviously, they didn't give our side of the story or even consider that this was out of our control. They had to blame someone, and it was us. At least now you get the full story.

❖ 2008 Presidential Election – Obama Campaign and Fake News

- To go along with the issues we had in dealing with the huge increase in student registrations the following occurred: because of the large number of students and parents calling us regarding their registrations I felt we should send out a press release to make students think about issues that they may not have considered before changing their registration. I took the exact wording from the State Board of Elections's website—word for word. As soon as I released it, I received a call from the Obama Campaign's attorney from DC. He immediately said I should withdraw the press release and said I was trying to keep the students from registering to vote. The *New York Times* article can be read through this link: *http://www.nytimes.com/2008/09/08/education/08students.html*. It was not long after this call that I started getting calls from the major newspapers and TV stations wanting a response. I tried to explain I was simply responding to the calls we received and trying to assist the students. At no time would we ever deny a qualified student to register with us. But these extensions of the Obama Campaign did articles and news stories that evening. The next morning, I got threatening phone calls from all over the country. The most vicious one came from Wyoming and he threatened to kill me.

  By the way, the two areas covered in the press release were the following: students needed to check with their scholarship donors to make sure by moving their permanent address to Blacksburg they would not lose it. The second issue involved health insurance. For example, it suggested that if the student was under the family's healthcare plan they should check with the provider to see if having a different address (Blacksburg again) would take them off the family plan. Both of these were important for the student to check. Two simple phone calls and they would be protected. I was trying to help them but got accused of trying to keep them from voting. If I was trying to do this, we would not have registered over 8,000 new registrants and a large majority of them living on campus.

As you could see from the *New York Times* article, the State Board of Elections said they would be changing their website. But that didn't matter, I was still the bad guy. Now this was a smart move on the part of the Obama Campaign. They found someone they could make out to be the bad guy and make them look good. But it was fake news. Think about it, they were tied to fake news back then!

❖ The *Roanoke Times* and Fake news regarding absentee ballots being sent out late

- Here is another fake news story being distributed by the *Roanoke Times'* reporter Christian Trejbal. Mr. Trejbal and I had a lot of issues over the time he was with the paper. He tried very hard with one article after another to get me fired. Fortunately for me my boards knew exactly what had happened and why things were being done. So, they always supported me, and Christian could never understand. When we first went to the touch screen voting machines, I invited Christian in to watch us program them for an election. He accepted my invitation and did an article saying Montgomery County's voting machines were protected. Unfortunately, he would not follow this approach in the future.

  This situation occurred due to miscommunication between the State Board of Elections and those of us across the Commonwealth. The Code of Virginia said that the absentee ballots were to be ready for voting forty-five (45) days prior to the election. The forty-five (45) days always ends up on a Saturday when our offices are not open. So, we always mailed out our absentee ballots on the following Monday. Well, when Ms. Nancy Rodrigues, SBE Secretary, came aboard she decided to take this literally and when we followed our regular routine, she made the announcement that several of us had missed the deadline. Nothing was said before this weekend, so we followed what we had done in the past. Once this was clarified with us, from that point forward everyone always made sure their absentee ballots were mailed on the forty-sixth day prior to the election. We were not alone; there were several jurisdictions across Virginia who mailed their absentee ballots out late. We checked after the election to make sure no one was affected by this and they were not. Christian blew up the story to attack me again.

❖ Christian Trejbal (The Roanoke Times) and ballot petition processing.

- Leading up to the 2010 Town Elections we obviously had to process the petitions for candidates so their names can be placed on the ballot. This election included the mayors for Blacksburg and Christiansburg. Each candidate must have a minimum of 125 certified signatures from voters within their respective towns. One important factor is that they must also be obtained within the calendar year of the election. This was very important in this situation and created quite an uproar with Mr. Trejbal and one of the candidates running for mayor. Since the elections were to happen in May, these candidates had to start collecting the signatures soon after the first of the year. One of the candidates for mayor of Christiansburg, Richard Ballengee, brought in his paperwork and petitions to be processed. I did what I always did and that was to hand the petitions over to my staff to check. In order to check the petitions, I had to use the other paperwork to set up the file in VERIS (Virginia Election and Registration Information System). Once this was done, the staff can then go into the system and check off the names. You should know that as soon as you hit the required number of signatures VERIS would not allow you check any more names. As soon as Mr. Ballengee hit that 125 signatures, he was certified as a candidate for mayor.

These petitions are open to the public to inspect and the candidate running against Mr. Ballengee came by to review the paperwork. A short time later, Mr. Trejbal came by and brought to my attention that several of the signatures certified had signed the petition prior to January 1, 2010, which would have excluded them from certification. I thanked him for bringing this to my attention and he asked what I was going to do. I told him I would be contacting State Board to determine what would be done and I would let him know the outcome.

I contacted Matt Abel at SBE to see what could be done. After discussing the situation, we decided the best action to take was to start over. In other words, Matt would eliminate Mr. Ballengee's certification and go back through his petitions and certify all of the signatures obtained after January 1, 2010. As promised I contacted Mr. Trejbal and told him what we were doing and that I would contact him once the certification process was over. Mr. Ballengee had several names still not checked so we did not know what the outcome would be. After my staff went through the names again, Mr. Ballengee still had enough names to be certified as a candidate. Again, as promised, I called Christian and told him the outcome. He was not happy with this and neither was the candidate who was opposing Mr. Ballengee. They attacked us viciously because they were hoping that their opposition would be eliminated.

My job as general registrar is to assist candidates and make it as easy as possible for them to get on the ballot. In this situation, no one was harmed. If VERIS allowed us to check all of the names to begin with it would have told us the total number of names he had, and we would not have had to check them again. Yes, we did not catch the dates of the signatures signed before January 1, we should have. When you are checking multiple petitions one after another you can miss something as small as this. The process for becoming a candidate is very hard and a lot of people do not run because of it. As I said, my job was to assist them getting on the ballot, not to prevent them.

So, I would take the hit for this decision. By the way, Mr. Ballengee won by a landslide.

❖ The Implementation of Electronic Pollbooks – Electoral Board Mistake

- I have already mentioned this earlier, but it needs to be addressed again. We had always used paper pollbooks, but the State Board of Elections was pushing us to change in order to speed up voter processing at the polls. After the huge lines in 2008, it was important to address them. SBE set up a program where we could get a used computer, software, routers, and cables needed for $100. This was quite a deal and we took advantage of it. We purchased seventy of them.

    After they were set up, we started the training of our officers of election. We had several training sessions, and everyone went through them. We even set up extra sessions in case someone still did not feel comfortable with them. Since the majority of our officers of election were over seventy years of age and many of them had no idea how to use a mouse, it was a challenge. But Gary Talkington and I felt they were ready.

    Unfortunately, some were not. Soon after 5:15 a.m. on Election Day, I started getting calls from chiefs indicating they were having problems getting the pollbooks up and running. Gary was out in the field and I sent him to the first ones that called. It turned out that a total of six (6) polling places out of our twenty-four (24) had issues and I helped many of them correct the problem by 6:00 a.m. when the polls were to open but not all. It is important to know that I was on the phone talking to one of the polling places when E-1, St. Michael's Lutheran Church, called in and asked what they should do. It was at this point that Cynthia Chappelka and Helen Young got together and decided to have them take everyone's name down on a legal pad. As I mentioned, this was not what they should have done. If asked I would have told them to give the voters a provisional ballot. In other words, they would be given a regular ballot and once marked, placed in a green envelope until the pollbooks were restored to determine if the voter was eligible to vote in that election and that precinct. This way we could verify their status. Unfortunately, I did not have the opportunity to address this issue, and as a result we all, the board and I, were sanctioned by the State Board of Elections.

I would not wish the experience of standing in front of the State Board of Elections on anyone. But our experience clarified what needed to be done when this happens, and it has.

❖ Nancy Rodrigues – Secretary from Hell

- As I mentioned earlier I met Ms. Rodrigues shortly after she was appointed by the Governor to her position as Secretary of the State Board of Elections (SBE). She traveled to Northern Virginia to VRAV's Annual Meeting to introduce herself to the GRs. This was the same meeting I was elected president of the organization. We met out in the foyer and she seemed to be very pleasant and she said the right things, i.e., I look forward to working with you to make our two organizations stronger; I am a team player and we will work closely together, etc. And for the first year this was the case. We had weekly teleconferences about issues concerning our business and on numerous occasions she would call me independently, even while I was in Walmart on the weekends, to address emergency situations across the Commonwealth. I felt we were accomplishing quite a lot and told the members of VRAV this. Then a little over a year into her tenure and halfway through my term, something happened. I don't know what led to this change, but it occurred just before the General Assembly started to meet and bills were being submitted for consideration. One particular bill got the attention of Alex Ables, Fauquier County General Registrar and member of the VRAV Legislative Committee. The bill was introduced by a legislator from Northern Virginia and would make all of the general registrars in the Commonwealth report directly to the secretary of the State Board. Alex brought it to my attention and I told him I would call Nancy and see what brought this about. When I spoke with Nancy about the bill, she said she knew nothing about it and would have to check with the legislator. I reported back to Alex with her explanation. Then a short time later we had one of our conference calls and she admitted that she had spoken to the legislator and asked him to submit the bill. In other words, she had lied to me. After the call I contacted Alex Ables and told him what I had just been told.

I then decided I needed to inform the entire association what had occurred. I wrote a letter to the members using the Association's letterhead explaining the timing of events. I didn't leave anything out. Obviously, this created a great divide between the SBE and VRAV. This divide continued throughout her tenure as secretary. VRAV's Legislative Committee worked very hard to defeat the bill in the General Assembly and were successful. So, Ms. Rodrigues' attempt to get control of VRAV was unsuccessful—thank goodness.

- Ms. Rodrigues's effect on the Department of Elections did not end when she left the Secretary's position. A Republican Governor was elected so she was replaced with a Republican. But four years later a Democratic Governor was elected, and he appointed Nancy as his Secretary of Administration—who coincidently had the Department of Elections reporting to her. She not only controlled the Department with an iron hand, but she would personally attend and run many meetings of the Department and the Commissioner of Elections would stand aside and let her lead. As in her tenure as Secretary, the staff were afraid for their jobs and would not speak up. They kept quiet and followed orders without question. She does not lead by example but with fear.

  VRAV still does not trust Ms. Rodrigues and is cautious when dealing with the Department of Elections, SBE, and her office. She has not changed and will not as long as she has control over that department. Since we have a new Democratic Governor, I am not sure if she is part of his administration.

CHAPTER THIRTEEN

What I Would Like for You to Get From this Book

Now that you know what general registrars/directors of election do, I hope you have a better understanding of what goes on behind the scenes during Election Day. I also wanted you to see the myriad of duties these outstanding professionals perform every day. They must be administrators, planners, trainers, librarians, computer experts, financial experts, psychologist, logistic experts, material managers, human resource professionals, and, above all, leaders.

I am proud to have been one of them and that they saw fit to allow me to be their president. This experience was more than I could have expected. I was able to learn how small, medium, and large localities operated, perceived our responsibilities, and managed their operations. I tried to lead with this information in my mind at all times. In other words, I tried to represent all localities regardless of size. I also got to meet a lot of wonderful people who are extremely dedicated to their profession and the fact that we are the "Defenders of Democracy." It is our responsibility to make sure qualified voters get to vote in all elections. We want to make sure the voices of the people are heard. By doing our duties we make sure this happens. This is quite a responsibility, they perform it well and need to be recognized for this remarkable performance. I am indebted to each of them for their knowledge, guidance, and friendship. Without it I would have not accomplished as much as I did. I grew in knowledge, experience, and appreciation for this profession.

Mostly, as the last part of the title of this book suggests, this group of professionals is totally underpaid for what they do. As mentioned in the "Prologue," I have considerable human resource experience and have developed many hourly and salaried pay programs. I have developed job descriptions and placed them on a pay scale according to their job duties and responsibilities. One of the major factors in this placement is what happens if this position makes a mistake. The general registrar's status is always placed too low by HR professionals who do not know what really goes on in our offices and during elections. If the GR makes a mistake during an election all heck breaks loose and the outcome of an election can be affected. Therefore, you can't get any more important than the actions of the general registrar. Appreciate your GRs/directors of election and recognize their contributions. As I said, they are the defenders of democracy and without them our democracy could be in jeopardy.

I have tried to show throughout this book the skills a general registrar/director of elections must have. Let me mention them again. A GR/director of elections must be able to do the following:

- Be a manager of the largest single-day workforce in Virginia, officers of election.
- Be an administrator
- Be a trainer
- Be an educator
- Be a student
- Be a receptionist
- Be a paralegal
- Be a file clerk
- Be a law clerk
- Be a policy analyst
- Be a department head
- Be a janitor
- Be an office administrator
- Be a financial analyst

- Be a data analyst
- Be a lobbyist
- Be an IT guru
- Be a systems administrator
- Be a secretary
- Be a Freedom of Information (FOIA) officer
- Be a human resources professional
- Be a boss/manager
- Be a campaign consultant
- Be a budget manager

These professionals also have unbelievable pressure on them to make sure every election goes smoothly. If one (1) officer of election out of your total of one hundred eighty-five (185) makes a mistake, it can become a major story on the news. As in one of my stories, an Electoral Board member makes a decision without consulting with the GR/Director of Elections, you can end up in front of the State Board of Elections and be censured. In a recent General Assembly Delegate Election in Virginia, a GR, who passed away, was blamed for redistricting errors and placing voters in the wrong district. Then after some investigation it was discovered that she had spoken with the Department of Elections (ELECT) about the issue and was told everything was okay. But the damage to the GR's reputation was already done. In other words, the GR/Director of Elections will always get the blame regardless of the situation. Therefore, we all use antacids and our nerves are totally shot around election time.

If these professionals were paid appropriately according to their responsibilities it would be one thing. But this does not happen throughout Virginia. Some smaller localities pay these professionals like a clerk in a library who has no responsibility. These individuals are taken advantage of and a lot of it is because of sexism. A large majority of the general registrars/directors of elections are female, and many county administrators/city managers view them as clerks. These leaders look at the position as simply a file clerk and, if everything goes smooth during an election, it is easy and only happens at most four (4) times a year.

As you know females have been underpaid over the years and have fought against this inequity for some time. I believe our salaries have been kept down because of this factor. When I first became the general registrar in 2004, you could count the number of males on one hand. At that time, we made up 3.7 percent of the GRs in Virginia. I checked with Rick Miller, VRAV Treasurer yesterday, and we now have twenty-two (22) male GRs or 16.5 percent.

It would be wonderful if these administrators/city managers would spend some time in our offices during a General Election, including Election Day. They would get a totally different impression and would not be envious of our responsibilities. But they stand back and go on what they think instead of what actually happens.

The one group that needs to be convinced is the General Assembly (GA). They set our base salaries in the annual budget. Yes, that is right. Our base salaries are set by a political body in their annual budget. We do not get a human resource professional to evaluate our positions like other state employees. Our salaries are determined when they balance the budget—many times on our backs. The GA members do this because we have no political power. There are only one hundred thirty-three (133) of us and these politicians ignore us. Even if you include VEBA, the total number of people affected is five hundred thirty-two (532) statewide. The GA members do not fear losing these few votes. Therefore, our salaries are kept low. Those who read this book, please see or contact your State Senator and Delegate and ask them to pay these professionals appropriately. They deserve the higher salaries due to their responsibilities, dedication, professionalism, and their role as defenders of democracy!

Hopefully, I have provided you with a clear understanding of what these great professionals do and how they accomplish their job duties. They are great individuals and patriots. The next time you get near their office, please drop by and say, "thank you." They will appreciate your understanding and support. If you really want to get involved in the political system and be a part of the defense of democracy become an officer of election. The GR/Director of Election would appreciate your help.

I am proud to have been a member of this family. Hope you have enjoyed this trip through history, my description of these great professionals, and my life as a general registrar/director of election. As you can see these professionals are overworked and underpaid.

ABOUT THE AUTHOR

E. Randall Wertz grew up in the small Southwestern Virginia town of Saltville and graduated from Virginia Polytechnic Institute and State University (Virginia Tech). He spent his professional career in the human resources field in state and local government, healthcare, and industry. Prior to becoming the General Registrar/Director of Elections in Montgomery County, Virginia, he also served as the Deputy Assistant County Administrator for nine years. He served as the General Registrar through four (4) Presidential Elections—two of which were the most controversial in US history.

He has been married to his wife, Mercedes, for thirty-nine years. She works for the Montgomery County Public Schools. They have a daughter, Kristina, who is a pharmaceutical sales person for a major drug company in Florida.